THE PROFESSIONALIZATION OF TEACHING

Is it Truly Much Ado About Nothing?

Robert P. Engvall

University Press of America, Inc.
Lanham • New York • London

Copyright © 1997 by
University Press of America,® Inc.
4720 Boston Way
Lanham, Maryland 20706

3 Henrietta Street
London, WC2E 8LU England

Library of Congress Cataloging-in-Publication Data

Engvall, Robert P.
The professionalization of teaching : is it truly much ado about
nothing? / Robert P. Engvall.
p.   cm.
Includes bibliographical references.
1. Teaching--United States. 2. Professional socialization--United
States. 3. Teachers--Training of--United States. 4. Teacher
effectiveness--United States. 5. Educational change--United States. I.
Title.
LB1775.2.E54   1996   371.1'02'0973--dc20   96-34222 CIP

ISBN 0-7618-0493-5 (cloth: alk. ppr.)
ISBN 0-7618-0494-3 (pbk: alk. ppr.)

♾™ The paper used in this publication meets the minimum
requirements of American National Standard for information
Sciences—Permanence of Paper for Printed Library Materials,
ANSI Z39.48—1984

Contents

Acknowledgments

The compilation of these thoughts into book form has required the patience and understanding of those who support my efforts. This includes my children Andrew and Benjamin, but most of all this includes Janet, without whom this work could not have been completed. I thank you Janet, for always standing by me in times of trial, and for sacrificing so much of yourself in order for me to pursue my dreams.

Chapter 1

Introduction

This introduction provides background information about the proliferation of school reform discussion that has resulted in, among other things, serious concerns about the quality and competency of teachers. The effectiveness of teachers has long been a public concern, but there has been an equally long reluctance to view teaching as a profession. Ultimately with a better understanding of teachers and their demands, might come positive reform or, at least, more skepticism toward uncertain reform proposals. Thomas Sowell (1995) writes about "prevailing vision" -- which he defines as the assumptions that many persons take for granted to such an extent, that the assumptions themselves are not generally confronted with demands for empirical evidence (p. 2). Schools and the teachers within them are often taken for granted to such an extent that assumptions about them and the work they do are often immune from evidentiary examinations.

"Teaching is a complex act, influenced by subtle conditions and swift teacher-student interactions" (Ornstein, 1995, p. 124). "Throughout the new paradigm on teaching, the centrality and wisdom of the teacher is reaffirmed, which is welcome and proper" (Ornstein, 1995, p. 128). If this is truly the new paradigm on teaching, challenging many of the assumptions that the public has about teachers and schools is of paramount importance.

Our collective view of unions has become increasingly negative and teachers' unions have suffered from this "prevailing vision." When we think of unions within the schools, we often think of organizations out to protect less than stellar teachers, and/or organizations out to raise our taxes in order to fund teacher salary increases. The positive impact of unionization is often, if not usually, overlooked. While it is difficult to argue against the merit of dismissing poor and ineffective teachers, it is equally difficult to argue with the mandates of due process and deliberate review.

School districts considering dismissal of a teacher should carefully review whatever procedures are contained within their personnel policies to make certain those procedures are followed. The issues of academic freedom, substantive and procedural due process, as well as any protected interests that may be violated, all need to be considered prior to making decisions about teacher dismissal.

"The citizen should become more informed on the operation of trade unions and collective bargaining. Since he or she will determine the ultimate status of unions, judgment as to their merits should be based on accurate information and sound analysis" (Taylor & Witney, 1992, p. 425). Taxpayers generally should find value in an assessment of the role of unionism in education in order to gain more understanding of the actual costs of teacher unionism. Parents should gain through better knowledge of what is expected legally and practically of their childrens' teachers. Further and most importantly, research has concluded that a teacher's faith in his or her ability to make a difference in a student does impact student achievement (Ashton & Webb, 1986; Glatthorn, 1992; Sergiovanni & Starratt, 1993). Such faith is often a product of the environment in the school. An efficacious teacher believes that he or she has the power and ability to produce a desired effect (Sergiovanni & Starratt, 1993). Several factors make it difficult for teachers to possess this sense of efficacy including: low pay, public criticism, limited collegial interaction, and the teachers' relative powerlessness within the organizational structure of the school (Glatthorn, 1992). The challenge for educators and for education is to find incentives that do not divide but instead bring about a collaborative search for better ways of coping with an extremely difficult set of problems (Bok, 1993).

Thus far, as this work considers more fully later, there has been an inability on the part of researchers to actually tie together collective bargaining with an improvement in student outcomes. By deduction, if it can be established that teachers' faith in their ability to make a difference improves student outcomes and teachers' "power," and that because of that their faith in their ability to make a difference within the structure of the larger school bureaucracy increases through their unionism and collective bargaining, then it may be possible to deduce that collective bargaining has a positive impact upon student outcomes.

For students of administration, there can be tremendous value in gaining a greater understanding of the profession generally, as it is, and as it might evolve. Such a greater understanding may be useful in assisting in some of the "subparts" of educational administration such as collective bargaining, professional ethics, and problem-solving within the schools on many levels. To study teachers, not by what they teach, but by what the "realities of teaching" are, and the level of "professionalism" that they have attained, administrators should be helped to better serve their staffs and ultimately improve the "atmosphere" to better promote higher levels of teaching and ultimately, higher levels of learning and consequently higher levels of community satisfaction. To complete the circle, such promotion of higher levels of community satisfaction might tend to improve community involvement and support of the public schools, which in turn would benefit all members of the school community, the administration, the teachers, and most importantly, the students.

The public's declining confidence in its schools has likely been the most significant reason for the voluminous literature concerning the issue of "school reform." For the purposes of this work, "school reform" refers to the overbroad, overvague concept of changing the present state of the schools. Teachers have allowed (probably through little fault of their own) "school reform" discussion to permeate the culture and climate surrounding the public schools. Within such a climate, it is easy to understand that organizations existing within that culture, such as teachers' unions, will undergo tremendous scrutiny and criticism, some fair, and some unfair. Whatever successes "unions" may have had in improving schools, the educational and mainstream press typically correlate union presence with labor conflict.

The aspiration to reform schools has been a recurrent theme in American education (Eisner, 1992). Retaining, or in some cases restoring, the public confidence in the schools is "essential for the continuation of the educational enterprise" (Wiles & Bondi, 1985, p. 215). Since the early 1980's, there have been numerous reports done by several persons and commissions all on the topic of "school reform" (see, for example, Adler, 1982; Boyer, 1983; Carnegie Task Force on Teaching as a Profession, 1986; Goodlad, 1984; The National Commission on Excellence in Education, 1983; Sizer, 1984).

For whatever reasons, taxes that go to social services such as "education" generally, and teachers' salaries specifically, are seen as more onerous than ever, and taxpayer revolt is becoming more and more common. The fact that fewer and fewer taxpayers have children in school and the increasing gap between the "haves" and "have-nots" are critical factors that have led to the erosion of widespread public acceptance of public education. A congressional study released in March 1989 shows that the average family income of the poorest fifth of the population declined by over 6 percent from 1979 through 1987, while the richest fifth saw their average family income rise by 11 percent (Chomsky, 1991). These tremendous and growing disparities between rich and poor make for an environment in which those at the top who control more and more wealth have little real stake in America's public educational system (Chomsky, 1991).

In this study the reform movement and its literature are seen through the lens of labor relations. A few others (notably Kerchner & Caufman, 1993) have attempted to put forth their own agenda for change (collaborative labor relations) through refocusing and redefining traditional perceptions about conflict-oriented labor relations. Kerchner & Caufman (1993) estimate that "collaborative labor relations" have been attempted in hundreds of school districts within the United States. Bascia (1994) also ably considers the impact of unions in the professional lives of teachers. This work attempts to put forth the proposition that rather than cloaking themselves in the "cover" of professionalism, teachers' associations would be better served by less argument over words and concepts, and more attention to the present realities of teaching.

The wealth of reform literature indicates, among other things, that schools no longer enjoy the community's unconditional trust and are frequently challenged to defend, in court and in the public debate, the decisions and actions of their boards and administrators. The extent to which education is genuinely valued in our society has often been called into question (Gardner, 1991). "The educational enterprise continues to be devalued by our society, our academic institutions, and even by us...part of the problem is caused by the simplistic way we think about it" (Weimer, 1993, p. 2).

> How can something so central to the mission of our institution, so intrinsically a part of the advancement of knowledge be given such short shrift? The answer is complicated, but I am firmly convinced that the lack of reward and recognition in part results from the simplistic, nonreflective, and uninformed ways many in our profession think about teaching. Approaching the teaching-learning enterprise in more intellectually robust ways puts you on the side of those of us committed to being part of the solution (Weimer, 1993, p. 124).

Faced with society's doubts about the public schools and the competence of those within the schools, administrators and boards have faced additional pressure to dismiss certain teachers. Within an evermore litigious society (Dunklee & Shoop, 1993), teachers, like other citizens, are increasing their willingness to question the decisions made by their employers when they feel that circumstances warrant such a challenge. Times like these require great vigilance to protect people's careers against any rush to action based on unstated values and presumptions rather than facts. "Fairness as well as effectiveness require that values be made explicit and that fact rather than assumptions be the basis for assessing blame for deficiencies in education and formulating solutions" (Gross, 1988, p. 2).

The increased "educational" litigation has heightened the need for legal assistance on the part of school districts and educators themselves. The fact that litigation is expensive, both in terms of dollars and time, is ample reason to avoid it at all cost. Beyond the expense, the publicity that school districts receive when they litigate against former employees is not usually favorable. Despite such knowledge, litigation does occur.

Chapter 2

"The Climate is Ripe, But the Fruit of Reform is Still Underdeveloped"

Fully 68% of persons responding to 1993's <u>Phi Delta Kappan/Gallup</u> poll, felt that the amount of money spent on a public school student's education either had "a great deal" or "quite a lot" of effect upon the quality of that student's education. Despite such sentiment, numerous studies have been unable to show a direct correlation between increased expenditures on schools and student performance (Finn, 1991). The most frequently cited conclusion of the well-known Coleman Report (Coleman, et al., 1966) is that differences among schools in the amount of money spent on education and even on teaching itself had little impact on student achievement. What did seem to make a difference was family background, social class, northern versus southern school location, urban versus rural school setting, and peer influence and traditions (Davis & Thomas, 1989). While conceding that "cultural deprivation and lack of stable family relations make the school's task more difficult," Dobay (1988, p. 51) states that "if smaller class sizes, better teachers, and more sophisticated resources would be extended to regular academic classes real progress might be made..."

The Coleman Report gave impetus to researchers to examine the effects of school climate. School climate was and is typically operationalized as the "expectations teachers have of students and students have of one another" (McDill and Rigsby, 1973; Holmes, 1971). There is considerable research on school climate, which "like the data on weather, is interesting, but inconclusive" (Holmes & Wynne, 1989, p. 233). Similarly, despite the best efforts of researchers, attempts to identify and define great teaching have been largely unsuccessful (Dobay, 1988). Little understanding of teaching resulted from studies that common sense had not already confirmed. "Good teachers are generally nice people who like students and derive much personal satisfaction from their work" (Dobay, 1988, p. 13).

One reasonable conclusion attained from the research is that higher teacher pay alone does not necessarily beget higher student performance. Weick (1976, 1982) found educational systems "loosely coupled" so that neither innovations nor additional resources produced the expected outcomes. Moreover, "a good teacher with or without a raise remains a good teacher. On the other hand, there are thousands of poor teachers who have remained poor teachers despite wage increases" (Rothman, 1977, p. 249). Teachers' working conditions likewise do not appear to logically relate to outcomes for children (Rutter, et al., 1979; Dunkin & Biddle, 1984). Rutter's study has been called the "single most influential study in the literature" (Holmes and Wynne, 1989, p. 254). Despite Rutter's standing, as with most statements made within the field, Rutter's is debatable. Boyer has stated that "improving working conditions is ... at the center of our effort to improve teaching. We cannot expect teachers to exhibit a high degree of professional competence when they are accorded such a low degree of professional treatment in their workaday world" (Boyer, 1983, p. 161; Goodlad, 1984). "Reform must begin with placing well-educated, effective teachers in classrooms and liberating them from the stultifying bureaucratic yoke which stifles their creativity" (Dobay, 1988, p. 44). Sergiovanni and Starratt (1993) conclude that "most policymakers agree that improving the teachers' workplace is one important way to improve schools." Gage (1978 & 1985) explained that even weak relationships between improvements for teachers and outcomes for students can make important differences.

The Climate of School Reform (Much Ado About Nothing)

In April, 1983, A Nation at Risk: The Imperative for School Reform, was published. So began the current school reform movement in earnest. The document was the work of the National Commission on Excellence in Education, a task force created by Secretary of Education Terence Bell, in 1981. The Commission's report dramatized what it considered the deteriorating quality of American education (Berube, 1988). "The rising tide of mediocrity" was the new phrase used to describe the public school systems. William T. Pink (1989) set forth two reasons for the importance of A Nation at Risk: (1) it reawakened the public interest in education in general and the importance of educational reform in particular, as it (2) set the agenda for subsequent reforms at the state and district levels (p. 123).

Although blaming the schools for the lack of achievement of many young people is easier and cheaper than blaming the society, it probably does little in the way of improving either society at large or the schools. Ernest Boyer (1983) suggests that blaming schools for the "rising tide of mediocrity" is to confuse symptoms with the disease. Whatever or whomever is to blame is substantially less important than a prescription for improvement.

The reform "movement" was dubbed the "excellence" movement, and for the most part, it placed the teacher unions on the defensive (Boyer, p. 127). President Reagan formally annointed the "excellence" movement in speeches after the report, proclaiming "American schools don't need vast new sums of money as much as they need a few fundamental reforms" (Ronald Reagan, "The President's Address to the National Forum on Excellence in Education," American Education, March 1984, p. 2). His use of the word "fundamental" was telling, as his belief of the need for restoring prayer, discipline, and parental involvement were loved by fundamentalists, and many others on the "right." In fairness, more than one side of the political spectrum has considered the merits of more parental involvement, particularly in support of "choice" measures (Gatto, et al., 1993). "Structurally, schools fly in the face of how children learn... it is not the fault of bad teachers, or of too little money spent"(p. 31).

The reform groups have generally interpreted "excellence" to mean such things as: raising academic standards; setting higher requirements for high school graduation and admission to college;

eliminating "soft" subjects: mandating a common core curriculum for all students; increasing math, science, and foreign language requirements; testing achievement regularly; lengthening the school day and year; and generally getting tough with students, teachers, and administrators (Passow, 1984, p. 674). While acknowledging the worthwhile goals, Martin (1989) views the "excellence" movement as an "elitist and class-biased corporate business perspective that, by its very structure, virtually dismisses an entire segment of the school population, those at the bottom of the social system" (p. 48). Popkewitz (1987) views the movements toward increased testing of teachers and students as a "ritual of differentiation and homogeneity"(p. 23), rather than a means to improve quality or standards in teaching or schooling. "Testing creates patterns of behavior that enable teachers and students to assume that there are universal meanings in experience" (Popkewitz, 1987, p. 23), or "objective knowledge and differences based solely on individual effort and merit"(Popkewitz, 1985, p. 349). "The discussion about excellence hides the ways in which the experiences of particular groups in society are given advantage through the development of particular dispositions, tastes, sensitivities, and awareness" (Popkewitz, 1985, p. 349).

The "excellence" movement shifted the public's attention to test scores as the primary means of assessing the quality of education (Burrup, et al., 1988), but the movement did little to actually "improve" the quality of education (St. John, 1992). A consensus is now emerging that a decade of top-down education reform has done little more than anger teachers and focus education on test-taking; it has not improved test scores and it has left teachers dissatisfied (Ginsberg & Barnett, 1990). Ten years after being forewarned of the nation's jeopardy, many critics assert that America's students still are not making the grade (Kantrowitz et al., 1993).

Not everyone agrees that the public schools are largely to blame for declining standards. According to Katznelson & Weir (1985), the broad ideological shift right in the early 1980's concentrated the public's attention on educational standards, rather than equality. Such an ideological shift naturally bred reports such as "A Nation At Risk"(1983).

Some educators have viewed the spate of reports bemoaning the poor academic quality of schools as entirely misplaced (Boyer, 1983; Spring, 1988; Urban, 1990). "These reports used the public schools as a scapegoat for larger economic problems caused by factors outside the realm of education" (Spring, 1988, pp. 58-9). Martin (1989) viewed the "excellence" movement as a name for a new tracking system for the best and the brightest. The public school system as, "the mainstay of the ideological state apparatus," would "more effectively legitimize and assist in the restoration and maintenance of a class-based heirarchical social system" (p. 54). Even among those who support greater "outside" participation by business and others, there is sometimes the acknowledgment that "schools replicate the social hierarchy that students bring with them" (Jones & Maloy, 1988, p. 20). Popkewitz (1985) views the social significance of the reform movements, and particularly the "excellence" movement, in the degree to which the symbols of change obscure the political interests served. "Concerns with equity and excellence are replaced with a singular call for excellence" (p. 349).

Perhaps, not surprisingly, the executive director of the NEA, blamed the Reagan and Bush administrations for "creating a political climate hostile to public education" (Cameron, 1992). Cameron (1992), described the "excellence" movement as "a seemingly genuine concern for improving public schools that has become an increasingly strident chorus arguing that public schools cannot be fixed."

> The irony of the fact that so many citizens have given up hope for public education and allowed once marginal issues to dominate the debate, is that the public schools remain one of the relatively most accessible institutions to democratic influence. And in fact the fight against public education is taking place in democratic and public forums. Schools are, after all, close at hand, less obscure and mysterious that a debate about NAFTA or even health policy. School issues can be seen and touched (Meier, 1995, pp. 79-80).

Whenever change or "reform" is contemplated in the public schools, teachers as the major "players" within the schools will be affected. We cannot study the effects of any "reform" that has not yet happened. Beyond reasoned guessing, we cannot know for certain what would be the end results of any number of reform proposals.

One of the reform movements of the 1980's and 1990's has been the effort to conceptualize education as a profession (Strike & Ternasky, 1993). Within the professionalism push is the view that teaching will be more effective if teachers are treated as professionals. Although the usefulness of the literature on professionalism is debatable, the concept of the professionalism of teaching has broader implications for society than higher test scores. Teaching Johnny to read and write, although extremely important functions of a school, may pale in comparison to what Johnny learns about society and its values from his time spent within the school. "Schools are expected to engage in the socialization of young children because of the relationship of socialization to social continuity" (Jarolimek, 1981, p. 5). Will Johnny learn to read and write more effectively if his teachers are better compensated? Will his experience be more positive if his teachers function in a "professional culture?" Since reform of the schools is receiving much attention, and many believe we are a nation still "at risk," a study of teachers themselves, and how their role in society is shaped by the courts, may begin to tell us more about what Johnny is actually learning in school. Schools, like all human inventions, change form either in reaction to social forces or because of our conscious attempt to change them and they communicate implicit as well as explicit messages to their students (Feinberg & Soltis, 1985). Mattingly (1987) calls the process of American education, "the process of socialization so selective and preferentially structured, the subordination of the teacher...clarifies much about the school as the balance wheel of the social machinery" (p. 51).

Beyer et al. (1989), make the claim that our present-day notions of profession are "inextricably bound to the division of labor"(p. 15). Since much of the debate over the quality or lack of quality in the public schools focuses upon teachers and their "professionalization," how "labor" in the form of teachers is perceived and how "labor" wants to be perceived directly ties "school reform rhetoric" to the realities for labor. Today, those realities usually involve collective bargaining.

In today's "reform" environment, large numbers of the public tend to believe, rightly or wrongly, that the schools aren't performing as they used to. Although what schools "used to do" is debatable, there is value in assessing the impact of a significant change that has taken place in schools within the last 20 to 30 years. Teachers now, in most states, have the right to collectively bargain their contracts for employment. Collective bargaining for public school teachers has been a change within the schools, the significance of which is, and has been, debated. Unlike other changes in schools that can be shrugged off as a reflection of society, for which the schools cannot be expected to bear sole responsibility (such as more violence), collective bargaining is a "concrete" change that should allow for research to more ably assess its impact.

The impact of collective bargaining as either an impetus for change, or an obstacle to it, is consistent with most educational research, inconclusive. "The collective bargaining process and resulting contract can either serve as one of the most effective vehicles for promoting and implementing educational reforms and change or as a major obstacle to change" (McDonnell & Pascal, 1988, p. x).

Chapter 3

"To Professionalize or Not to Professionalize,That is the Question"

This chapter proposes that educators might thoughtfully reexamine the increasingly "accepted orthodoxy" of increased "professionalism" for teachers. While many, if not most, aspects of greater "professionalism" for teachers are legitimate means by which to improve the delivery of education, as well as the status of teachers, the tendency among educators to seek greater professionalism by comparing ourselves to the more established "professions" may be wrongheaded.

> Teaching is a social practice whose importance is unquestioned, even if what makes it important remains the subject of continued debate (Hansen, 1994, p. 266).

The importance of "good" teaching is difficult to question. The problem for teaching as a "profession," is in coming to grips with the exact nature of what it is that "good" teachers do, and how "good" teaching as either a science, an art, or a combination of both can effectively be transmitted to prospective teachers. Among the problems the "profession" of teaching has in transmitting this knowledge is the extremely high value (appropriately or not) placed upon experience as a guide to "good" teaching.

This chapter considers the well entrenched theory that holds:

since "good" teaching is extremely difficult to predict or even define, it must consequently be experience, rather than scientific theory, that is the best guide. Whether such a "trial and error" approach is positive for our children is perhaps the most important issue such an approach presents, but another issue lies in the lack of "professional" status that such an approach surely conveys.

Our colleges of education routinely seek teacher-educators who have had experience within the public schools. From such requirements flows the logic that "poor" or at least "less good" teachers of teachers are apparently readily recognizable as those who haven't taught in schools before. Which then leads to a concern about the "professional" inconsistencies of teaching, and the dangers of such a unique vocation using the more traditional and established professions as models.

If education "professionals" at the collegiate level must have had experience (usually the magic number is three years) in teaching at the elementary or secondary level, it must follow that "good" teachers become "good" teachers more through experience, than through education. This theory begets a painful and somewhat hypocritical reality. That reality is that teaching is far more an art than a science, and since most education professionals might stammer when confronted with the question "What makes a good teacher," why then do these same education professionals propose to know how to teach others to become "good teachers," or better yet, how do these same persons propose to know who will not prepare "good teachers?" Attempting to reconcile this "need" for experience with the desire, on the part of so many educators, to achieve greater "professionalization," modeled mostly after the traditional professions of law and medicine, leads necessarily to the conclusion that the entire "professionalization" debate needs significant further assessment at best, and is entirely misplaced at worst.

However valid teachers' concerns are over low pay, and low status, there must be a better way to achieve these things than to continually assert the similarities between teaching and other professions, since whatever the quality and quantity of the similarities, it is the differences that are the most striking. These differences mandate a reassessment of the goal of greater "professionalization," at least in terms of the type of "professionalism" exhibited by some of the more established "professions."

Is Teaching an Art, a Science, or a Calling?

Booth (1988) describes teaching as "the most difficult and important of all the arts. Like all arts, it surely must depend in part on knowledge, but like all arts it depends on knowledge that is elusive, manifold, and resistant to clear formulation" (p. 210). Booth is not alone in his view that teaching is more art than science: "We are in sympathy with the general thrust of the notion that teaching is a craft rather than a science or discipline" (Holdaway, 1994, p. 208). Lieberman and Miller (1978) likewise believed that "the vague goals of teaching (such as individualize and teach everyone in the class) along with the ambiguous connection between what is taught and what is learned, require artistry, as opposed to scientific thought" (p. 56).

Hansen (1994) goes beyond the art/science debate entirely to describe teaching in terms of the ancient religious and the more modern secular use of the word "vocation." To Hansen, teaching, rather than a choice of careers, is more in line with a "calling." "An individual who is strongly inclined toward teaching seems to be a person who is not debating whether to teach but rather is contemplating how or under what circumstances to do so" (Hansen, 1994, pp. 266-67). Hansen also acknowledges that many receive "the call" after beginning careers in other fields.

> To describe the inclination to teach as a budding vocation also calls attention to the person's sense of agency. It implies that he or she knows something about himself or herself, something important, valuable, worth acting upon. This suggests that one conceives of teaching as more than a job, as more than a way to earn an income...but as potentially meaningful, as the way to instantiate one's desire to contribute to and engage with the world (Hansen, 1994, p. 267).

Is a "calling" compatible with "professionalism?"

Educational researchers frequently compare teachers' work with the kinds of work performed in other occupations (Rowan, 1994). In these analyses, teaching is usually seen as a form of professional work, that is, a type of complex work requiring a great deal of specialized knowledge (e.g., Sykes, 1990). However true it may be that teaching is complex, the widely accepted notion that teaching is, to some degree at least, a "calling," leads to the inescapable conclusion that comparisons to "accepted professions" such as law, are inappropriate at best. While not my purpose to berate lawyers, it is relatively rare that a person enters law school to either "see justice done" or to "change society." According to the ABA Journal (September 1986) the reasons more than half of the practicing attorneys who responded to that particular poll recall being attracted to law school was because "the subject interested them" or "their work as lawyers would be interesting." Even less in line with a "calling," 46% said they chose law because of "income potential," and 43% listed the "prestige of a legal career" (See also Moll, 1990, p. 25). However valid these notions, we might be disturbed if such numbers were true of teachers. How would teachers feel if 46% of their colleagues said they chose teaching because of "income potential?" More important than how teachers might feel, how would parents feel if income potential was known to be a prime motivator of those who became the teachers of their children?

Efforts to compare teaching with other occupations are often not efforts to logically analyze the professions, but are rather rooted in broader concerns about the professional status of teaching. Although education workers in the U.S. have been trying to professionalize the occupation of teaching since at least the turn of the century, most observers agree that this project has been only partially successful (Rowan, 1994). Aside from the limited success of the effort to "professionalize" teaching, there is a fairly significant debate over the value of the "professional" label itself. "Broad labels such as profession, craft, or labor often conceal as much as they reveal, especially when used to describe the nature of work performed by a given occupation" (Rowan, 1994, p. 5).

Others more simply believe that whether or not teaching is a "true" profession it is not (and will not be) viewed as a profession because the complexity of teaching is hidden beneath the apparent simplicity of its execution and because it is not cloaked in unfamiliar language (Goens & Glover, 1991; Bacharach, et al., 1990). "As sociological research on work and occupations demonstrates, the prestige and earnings that accrue to an occupation depend to a significant extent on the complexity of the work performed by that occupation" (Rowan, 1994, p. 13). Freidson (1986) similarly wrote about the "mystification of knowledge" that the established professions have been able to enjoy both through their own good fortune and their intentional and careful cultivation. Such a "mystification of knowledge" that has accrued to the benefit of the legal and medical "professions," runs counter to the long-term goal of educators, which is and should be the de-mystification of knowledge. Seeking greater involvement in the education of children by parents, and the community as a whole, is almost universally seen as beneficial (see among others, Crowson, 1992; Wanat, et al., 1994).

Teaching's claim to professional status, is grounded in the following reality: Teaching children and adolescents is complex work, and successful performance of this work requires high levels of general educational development and specific vocational preparation (Rowan, 1994). Assuming we accept this, then the question is not whether teachers should be afforded the status of doctors and lawyers, but rather "what meaning should teachers and non-teachers alike attach to the profession of teaching?"

Does "Professionalism" Accrue Without Cost?

Assuming, as many do, that teaching will only be improved, (however vague that term is) by its greater acceptance as a "profession" in line with the more established "professions," then will such improvement come without cost? There has been no shortage of literature about "professionalism," and if that literature is judged by its lack of real and measurable impact, it is arguable that too much has already been written about "professionalism" generally, and the "professionalization of teaching" specifically. By the mid to late 1980's, professionalism was becoming a tired subject for many education authors, i.e. Ginsburg (1987). Yet despite the "tiredness" of the subject, the value of the debate remains if only because the resolution of the problem has not yet arrived.

While much has been written extolling the virtues of "professionalism" and the term itself conjures up almost exclusively positive connotations, little has been written suggesting that the "need" to "professionalize" teaching comes at a significant cost. Notable among the few "doubters" has been Ayers (1992) who warned of the dangers thusly: "if teachers see professionalism as a type of elitism separating them from the community at large, a successful 'partnership' among teachers, parents, administrators, and the community will be more difficult" (p. 24). While little argument exists among most members within the teaching profession who would presumably like to see the income and status of teachers raised, the impact of and subsequent dangers of seeking greater "professionalism," at least in terms of what "professionalism" has commonly meant, have been largely ignored.   Foremost upon those list of dangers lies the detachment requirement that "professionals" need to embody, and which their respective "professions" require.

Among many theorized dangers of "professionalization" are the tendency to serve the profession first, to believe the ideology, to utilize the mythology, separate the people, mystify the knowledge, protect secrets, abuse power, and avoid responsibility (Kraybill & Pellman Good, 1982; Andrews, 1992).   While each of these elements may be harmful in themselves, perhaps the most relevant as far as teaching is concerned lies in the tendency of "professionals" to distance themselves from their work.   Such distancing naturally comes at the expense of creating quality personal relationships.

In seeking greater "professionalization" through attempts to compare teaching with the more commonly accepted "professions," there is a tendency to ignore the negative elements that might come along with the positive elements in the rush to achieve the status and recognition commonly afforded the more accepted professions. Since teaching kids and young adults is vastly different from performing surgery, diagnosing individual patient or client needs, and most, if not all other aspects of law and medicine, there should be a certain amount of trepidation that comes along with comparing "apples and oranges." So far, however, there has been little reluctance on the part of teachers and teachers' organizations toward proposing greater "professionalization." Such a full speed ahead approach has led to a diminishment in the analysis of any potential costs, as most of the literature simply compares and contrasts teaching with the more established professions, while largely ignoring the differences in the ultimate "product."

Lost for the most part in the desire to professionalize, is the recognition that professionalism (at least in the traditional sense) would mean greater detachment. Such greater "professional" detachment is difficult to perceive of as better for students' needs. Many educators have ably focused upon the need for "attachment" and caring, as opposed to detachment.   Ayers (1992) specifically decried professionalism if it were to mean "an overemphasis on developing a 'knowledge base' for teaching and a corresponding weakening of attributes like compassion" (p. 24). Mem Fox (1993) perhaps put it best:

"I see no age difference in the fundamental need for good relationships in teaching/learning situations; I believe they arise from knowing those whom we teach and knowing those who teach us: from being open about our lives and our own outside-school realities, and from caring about and knowing the different people in our classes" (p. 78).

While many of Mem Fox's reflections specifically concern reading, her thoughts are equally appropriate to learning in general. "I'm certain that learning to read and learning to love reading owe a great deal (more than we ever dreamed) to the nature of the human relationships that occur around and through books" (Fox, 1993, p. 136). It is the human relationships that occur between teacher and student that create within the student an interest in learning that might continue beyond the teacher-student contact. Just as parents attempt to instill within their children security, love, and independence, so too should teachers attempt to instill within their students the security of a good learning environment, love of the subject, and the independence to continue learning long after the class is over. Success as a teacher must necessarily lie in fostering the human relationships in which the teacher and the student are allowed to follow their natural inclinations in a classroom. These natural inclinations usually follow the path of teacher as leader and students as followers of that lead. To effectively teach all our students requires that we acknowledge the differences between and among our students, and treat them as individuals that we care about. The detachment of the "professions" runs counter to such involvement. To ignore the differences and promote the pretense that all students can master the same curricula and the same standards "professionally" taught will force a real decline in the quality (however measured) of our schools.

School improvement requires systemic change in teacher improvement and equalized school capacity, not higher content and performance standards (Darling-Hammond, 1994). It is the "large inequalities in opportunities to learn that are more responsible for learning gaps than a paucity of tests" (Darling-Hammond, 1994, p. 478). Any attempts to increase the "opportunities to learn," aside from the useless rhetoric coming from Congress and most state legislatures, must at base focus upon teachers and their interactions with individual students.

Another potential pitfall of "copycat professionalism" lies in the difficulty accepted autonomous "professionals" often have in working together toward a common goal. "A profession that derives its authority and its influence from the fact that people need its services can become exploitative unless its members possess a high degree of altruism and work together to promote and foster high ideals in themselves and in their colleagues" (Curtin, 1994, p. 32). "Professionalism" for teachers depends in large part upon the trust that teachers are able to justifiably evoke from the parents of their students and from their students themselves. Anything less than this type of "caring professionalism" such as the detached "uncaring professionalism" exhibited by doctors and lawyers, is inappropriate for teachers, if not morally, then simply because of the nature of their work.

Since "good teaching" is so difficult to define with any certainty, the ability of education detractors to bemoan the state of education and their accompanying pleas to overcome "poor teaching" and poor student outcomes continues to mount. Since we societally, are reluctant to blame ourselves for the short-comings, real or perceived in others or often even ourselves, many have latched onto teachers as the scapegoats for poor educational outcomes, high drop-out rates, and a general and undefinable lessening in our "values." Because teachers are accessible and, as of yet, have not effectively raised their voices in outrage against such blame, they continue to be perceived not only as passive, but as accepting of the criticism as implied by their relative silence.

Many inside and outside of the education "establishment" have proposed "solutions" to the problems confronting teacher education programs. Whether these reformers feel a real need to overcome teacher deficiencies or merely to placate the public is debatable, but in any case, many proposals have been cast out to test the waters of public and legislative opinion. "Recent policy proposals for reforming teacher preparation have highlighted once again apparent limitations of teacher education and problems associated with initiation to teaching" (Holdaway, et al., 1994, p. 205). Proposals ranging from greater teacher autonomy to increasing and tightening standards to which teachers should be held, allow for a wide variety of criticisms directed at schools generally and teachers primarily. Even those who generally are supportive of teachers often add to the assumption that teachers are doing a poor job through their proposals that aim at teachers, rather than at schools and/or the negative influences of poverty, crime, and other mountainous obstacles that many children face.

Blaming the teachers has been popular not only with critics on the "outside," but often with critics "inside" schools, colleges of education and other would-be "teacher sympathizers." Suggestions such as internships for beginning teachers, which may or may not prove valuable, do suggest a certain amount of fear of the damage that might be caused by beginning and inexperienced teachers. "Internships may play a significant role in developing competencies on the job and facilitating the transition from university student to full-fledged professional. By overcoming the disjunction between theoretical education and practical preparation, internship programs may ultimately prove to be an important vehicle for enhancing the quality of teaching" (Holdaway, et al., 1994, p. 219). Whether or not internships, as an example, would "improve" teaching, the implied assumption is that poor teaching is at the heart of the problems facing schools.

Conclusion

As is the case with so much of the education literature in particular, and social science literature in general, this chapter proposes little in the way of solutions, but instead hopes to promote further consideration of a complex concept (professionalism) that heretofore has been mostly lauded without great depth of analysis. This article is intended to foster further debate over the merits or demerits of greater professionalism for teachers. Ultimately, while greater professionalism is appropriately pursued for many reasons, we will be better served by recognizing that proper professionalism for teachers and teaching must not embody "copycat professionalism," but an entirely new type of professionalism. One that encompasses much of what law and medicine have traditionally stood for, but also one in which many of the "requirements" of the more established professions are properly rejected. Sykes (1989) viewed the proper goal for teachers as not a position among the high professions, which he viewed as quite unlikely, but merely a more manageable improvement in their status. Herbst (1989) similarly concludes that teachers "can and should develop their own professionalism, not an imitation of the professionalism of doctors, lawyers and school administrators, but through their own indigenous professional conduct in the classroom" (p. 196).

While all professions have their inconsistencies, teaching as a profession, at least in the traditional sense, is frought with them. Unlike teaching law or medicine, teaching education at the collegiate level seems to require previous experience teaching much younger children.

Such an informal "internship" seems to run contrary to the "science" of the more traditional professions which allow "practice" after completion of satisfactory entrance examinations, without great regard, especially in the case of the law, to practical experience in the field. If teachers and teachers of teachers feel that their programs are more important than law or medicine, and therefore might require a satisfactory internship program to minimize potential harm to future students, then so be it. If that is the case however, then comparisons with law and medicine seem to be inappropriate.

Moreover, however easy it may be to simply compare teaching with law and medicine, and then attempt to validate such comparisons in the hope of attaining some of the status that the two more accepted "professions" have been afforded (both rightly and wrongly), it is wrongheaded and would ultimately be both disappointing for our students and less fulfilling for ourselves. One should only have to attend one conference in which many lawyers are gathered to conclude that "being more like lawyers is not in the best interests of teaching, or of students." While exceptions to the generalization abound, "lawyer in America has come to connote egoism and rabid competitiveness coupled with greed, a seeming detachment from issues of right and wrong, and one who is very bright and hardworking but, so often, dull" (Moll, 1990, p. 3). If this is the "professional" model that teachers aspire to, they should pause and deliberate carefully, for after true "professionalism" is attained, it will take a long time for the student/teacher and teacher/parent relationships to adjust. The adjustment may well be more damaging in the long term than education can bear.

"The phenomenon of learning takes place in diverse ways, and we'd be fooling ourselves if we believed it happened only when we 'teach' in the narrow sense. Our ultimate success as teachers can't really be measured until our students have left us. If, in their continuing lives, our past students can deal confidently and competently with any real (situation) only then can we claim to have taught them well" (Fox, 1993, p. 109). Confidence and competence may best be instilled through positive teacher-student relationships, in which students feel certain that their teachers actually "care" about their success. In this age, when more and more students come to school carrying a heavy burden of social and emotional baggage, it is even more important that teachers not lose sight of their obligation to "care." Such an obligation should carry much greater status than our society has afforded teachers, but casting aside that obligation will do great and lasting harm to the "profession" of teaching, and more painfully still, to the students themselves.

Chapter 4

More Standards, Less Autonomy or More Autonomy, Fewer Standards, Perhaps That is the Question.

Teachers find themselves caught between two opposite extremes. One side of the spectrum views them as professionals in need of more "professionalization," while the other suggests the need for more direct supervision, more stringent state licensure requirements, and more adherence to "standards." Timar and Kirp (1988, p. 75) suggest that "the school reform movement is peopled at one extreme by hyperrationalists who believe that schools are infinitely manipulatable, and at the other extreme by romantic decentralizers who believe that if left alone schools will flourish."

"In today's schools it is common for teachers to be regulated and controlled by an elaborate work system which specifies what must be done and then seeks to ensure that it is done. When this is the case, the work of teachers becomes increasingly bureaucratic. But bureaucratic and professional work are different" (Sergiovanni & Starratt, 1993, p. 67). Bureaucrats are subordinate to the system, while professionals are superordinate to their work system (Sergiovanni & Starratt, p. 67). The increasing tendency to refer to teachers as "professionals," while considering their work to be bureaucratic, has been a source of puzzlement to both teachers and the public. The recent debate about education reform in schools can be seen as a debate between two different logics of action -- the bureaucratic logic of accountability and the professional logic of autonomy (Bacharach & Conley, 1989). Thus far, there has been no evidence to indicate that a satisfactory reconciliation to this dilemma is forthcoming.

The desire to find out what is "wrong" with the schools; why test scores are declining; why schools seem ineffective in controlling violence and vandalism, teenage pregnancies, and drug abuse, motivates those "in charge" to hold teachers accountable to the taxpayers and funding agencies for the money they spend (Sergiovanni & Starratt, 1993). Others want to find out what is "wrong" in order to increase information about successful programs and teachers in order that more may learn by example. Whether one is motivated by a desire to hold schools "accountable," or to point out the "good" that schools do, evaluation of the present conditions and circumstances within the schools leads logically to evaluation of the persons within the school.

In any profession or vocation, there are persons who become subject to review and occasionally, subject to dismissal. The field of education does not differ in that most practitioners are quite able, while some, however few and for whatever reason, are not. "Every school system needs a rigorous teacher evaluation system that ensures that incompetent teachers who do not demonstrate the capacity for growth are professionally terminated" (Glatthorn, 1992, p. 62).

The legality of the contract between school boards and teachers is affected by not only the usual basic requirements of any contract, but also statutory guidelines. In many cases, personnel practices that had become institutionalized through custom have been challenged as being discriminatory, violative of statutory or constitutional provisions, or simply as unfair (LaMorte, 1992). Although teachers are not always successful in court actions, their increased willingness to employ the courts has produced a climate, generally, in which school boards and school administrators have become more sensitive to the necessity of treating teachers in a legally defensible manner (LaMorte, p. 189).

All states have enacted statutes relating to teachers. Failure to live up to the statutes, and indeed the expectations of the employing school district, leads to, or may lead to dismissal. The actual dismissal process is different in different states, but ultimately the purpose is the same, to rid the school district of a given teacher.

Teachers are dismissed for a variety of reasons. The power of boards to dismiss teachers from employment has diminished with the passing years as more attention has been paid to state statutory provisions and constitutional protections. Not everyone has been enamored with the increase in teacher "power." As early as 1971, prior to collective bargaining in most states, some authors expressed concerns over the increasing power of teachers, and the accompanying decrease in "power" of administrators (Lewis, 1971). It is unclear how much of that "power shift" was due to an improvement in the quality of teachers, of more and better tenure laws, of support for teachers from teachers' organizations, and from the ongoing evolution of society.

Since public schools are taxpayer supported, the perceptions of the public outside of the school are critical to the success of the venture not only in willing taxpayer support, but also in terms of the involvement of the community in desiring a "successful" school, and a subsequent showing of support by actions as well as money. "Because tax dollars pay for public education, many Americans feel that schools belong to them" (Dobay, 1988, p. 14). Largely because of this "ownership" public schools are highly susceptible to political pressures. Parents, businesspersons, politicians, and other interest groups have all attempted, and still attempt, to influence decisions made by educators. These "pressured" teachers work under the auspices of a wide variety of formal political authorities, including legislatures, school boards, and state and local bureaucracies. Individual teachers then cannot avoid exercising political power, whether that power is their own or that of those who direct their actions (Bull, 1993). There is an interesting tendency among many Americans to practice "selective ownership" over public ventures. The ownership is selective because our citizenry demands accountability over the spending of "their tax dollars" when these dollars go toward social services such as education, welfare, or healthcare; yet there is little demand for accountability and concern over "ownership" when many more tax dollars are spent on the military, or on savings and loan bailouts. Because of our knowledge that much public money is wasted, we seem to demand accountability for social service spending, yet despite this same knowledge we tend to advocate greater military spending with little reservation and with little political opposition. Newspaper and television accounts of "welfare cheats" tend to capture the public's imagination and the public's outrage, while similar stories of corporations cheating the government over defense contracts is more or less brushed aside as "the cost of doing business."

In this complex climate of "concern," both inside and outside the highly political organizations in which public schools exist, there is a blurring of reality and perceptions. Teachers appear to the nonteacher world to be people of authority, legal sanction, license, and influence. But teachers often believe themselves to be powerless, abused, underpaid, and generally unappreciated (Ayers, 1992). This disparity in perceptions has created a climate that has allowed fertile ground for misunderstanding and mistrust on both sides.

There have been comprehensive studies of the impact of collective bargaining on the economic and professional status of teachers, probably the most comprehensive of which is that carried out by RAND's Center for Policy Research in Education. In 1979, RAND researchers concluded that in the first decade of substantial bargaining (1970-1979), teachers made substantial gains in improving their working conditions by expanding their influence over the length and composition of the school day, the manner of teacher evaluation, and the use of supplementary personnel (McDonnell & Pascal, 1979). During the 1980's, according to these same researchers, teachers continued to expand their sphere of influence (Keith & Girling, 1991). If there is no dispute that teacher influence has expanded since the advent of collective bargaining, the dispute remaining lies in the quantity and quality of that expansion, and what impact that expansion has had, if any, upon schools.

To find an answer, or at minimum to better understand any answers once they are found, it is imperative that we examine teachers' defining organizations, the NEA and the AFT, and in the context of these associations discover what effect there has been on teacher dismissal cases. Assessing any gains they have made within one narrow area may shed light upon how they might achieve further success or, in the alternative, lead to a questioning of the worth of these organizations. Further, the overall "climate of reform" in which the public schools are perceived as somehow deficient has played a significant role in the status of public school teachers and is a cloud hovering over the landscape on which teachers work and from which public perceptions are formed. The "problem" for teachers lies in the decline of the "profession," whether real or perceived, as a result of the "climate of reform." Only by a shift in the paradigm that views schools as deficient and failing and in need of "reform," toward a view of schools as largely positive places in need of some relatively minor adjustments, can the status of teachers in our society be significantly improved.

Whenever a segment of society is generally criticized, as

teachers have been, any veil of secrecy or mystery that may have shrouded that segment is lifted as different interest groups rise to the defense or the prosecution. When teaching as an occupation is analyzed, the issue of teacher professionalization inevitably follows. Assessing the behavior and/or ability of teachers as professional persons subject to certain standards is one of the most serious problems that school administrators and boards face. The labor relations perspective is important because unions are, or can be, powerful influences on teachers' work lives and school operations, and labor relations provide a particularly revealing outlook on educational change (Kerchner & Caufman, 1993). Neither unions nor schools can change without the other changing too. Unions alone cannot empower teachers to reorganize schools, to impose professional standards, or to increase student achievement. Likewise, managements alone are incapable of reorganizing schools, changing their schedules, or altering the duties of employees (Kerchner & Caufman, 1993, p. 2).

Chapter 5

The Law and Education

The law and its influence in education, like other subjects, should be studied within the context of time, place, and dimension. By its nature, the law is interpretive, requiring certain decision-making assumptions over which reasonable persons may, and often do, strongly differ. Discretion in educational decision-making is important to the educational process and has usually been given wide latitude in the courts. In order to obtain value from this or any study, the reader needs, as always, to understand the total environment in which the study was made and from which the study cannot be separated. Although the narrow problem has been stated, and the narrow focus of research has been stated, such a study without a foundation of the environment in which teachers and collective bargaining as entities coexist would be diminished in value. To that end, the ensuing discussion of school "reform" and "professionalism" in education are vital to a broader understanding of the ultimate conclusions of this study. Without them the study still exists as a valid undertaking and the data collected serves a purpose, but with the understanding of the wider environment surrounding "professionalism" and "reform" in education, the study takes on greater value as a "truer" indication of the teaching "profession" today.

It seems fair to date the contemporary educational "reform" movement to the publication of A Nation at Risk in 1983 (See among others, Urban, 1991; Finn, 1990; Goodlad, 1990; Kerchner & Caufman,

1993). Any fair assessment of that document, and others of that era, must consider the larger political climate which allowed for their creation. During the 1980's and the administrations of Reagan and Bush, it takes no great thought or imagination to describe the political climate as one in which the words and concepts "unions" and "government" were usually described in negative ways. Education policies were advanced that actually sought privatization and voucher programs to make it "easier" for parents to send their children to private rather than public schools. In such an era, it is only fair to point out as too few have done (Urban, 1991), that many of the school "reformers" had goals other than public school improvement. In fact, they may have had political reasons for accentuating the flaws within the public schools, and for putting forth to the public at large that the public schools were sinking ships. In the pages that follow, this study will attempt to help dispel the myth that unions and collective bargaining have "harmed" the public schools.

The difficult problems schools face today have been frequently addressed in the literature. Likewise, as is a recurrent theme in this research, literature on "reform" is abundant. Nevertheless, "reform" seldom happens, and what "good reform" should be is difficult to agree upon. If the literature has not helped to "solve" the many problems schools face, then it needs to be understood in that context. Further, the value of the wealth of literature is doubted even by those within the profession (Latham, 1993).

One purpose of this chapter is to provide enough of a history and "feel" for the evolution of teachers' organizations to benefit the reader in assessing the role these organizations play today. This chapter discusses the literature as it portrays the major issues concerning and surrounding teacher dismissal. Specifically, this chapter investigates areas related to school board policy, tenure, teacher professionalism/unionism, teacher licensing, teacher malpractice, the evolution of the "profession," and the expectations of society.

In today's world, when a tenured or "continuing contract" teacher is dismissed "for cause," the courts often become involved. The historical reluctance by the courts to enter the "school policy" arena, while still present, has diminished. Depending upon one's perspective, no longer can school boards exercise dictatorlike power, or no longer can the "dirty laundry" of schools be washed privately, at least without the consent of the parties. In any case, the emergent law resulting from court decisions themselves, as well as the law for which decisions provided great incentives for legislation, now greatly impacts educational policy. A review of the literature indicates, quite clearly, that there is much concern about the quality of public education. Within that concern, necessarily, lies the public interest in seeing that ineffective teachers are removed as efficiently as is possible. It is with that background, that this literature review will now specifically address the areas relating to the dismissals of tenured teachers, and illustrate the larger context and climate from which the cases studied have arisen.

Giving Schools the "Business"

Perhaps the most significant aspect of the 1980's and the "excellence" movement, in terms of this study, was the increased involvement of business in the public schools. The public debate about the nature of schooling had been replaced by the concerns and interests of management experts (Giroux, 1988). The politics of those behind the "excellence" movement might diminish the significance of their support of business involvement. Much of the "effective schools" literature, however, also supports greater involvement of business within the public schools (Boyer, 1983; Goodlad, 1984;Davis & Thomas, 1989). Wise (1981) urged businesses to ask how schools can be more responsive to the needs of employers and to examine joint "educational functions of both schools and employers" (p.79).

Many critics (Timpane, 1984; Martin, 1989; Sola, 1989), question the right of these "interest groups" to define the "public interest"- especially if the "public interest" is one of self-interest. Ironically, for this study, as unions were being derided as self-interested "special interests," corporations were invited in to the school reform debate as a way of focusing schools on America's declining economic prosperity and productivity.

Whether or not businesses lent "aid and comfort" out of self-interest, or out of altruism, the fact is that educators and businesspeople have great difficulty genuinely communicating with each other (Graham, 1992). "School people are often either intimidated or irritated by self-assured business leaders who... tell them how to organize themselves and how to run their institutions more efficiently and competitively. Successful businesspeople, on the other hand, are appalled at the bureaucratic rigidities and administrative sluggishness besetting schools" (Graham, p. 138). Sarason (1984) saw the failures of school-business partnerships arising from the occasioning of "two cultures misunderstanding and clashing with each other" (p. 19).

The danger of somehow equating public schooling with running a business lies in the input/output dependance of business thought, and the inability to transfer input/output dependance to the public schools. The business involvement tends to focus the success or failure of any reform initiatives on a measure of inputs vs. outputs. This approach fails to recognize that the wisdom and accuracy of measuring "human outputs," as the production unit of schools, is highly questionable.

The Persistence of and Abundance of "Reform"

Calls for "reform" of the public schools are far from new. Charles Silberman (1970) found that despite uncounted reform attempts, "the schools themselves are largely unchanged" (p. 159). "For all the palaver over education, one is struck not by the immediacy or novelty of the debate but, in the context of the last thirty years, by the seemingly persistent dissatisfaction with the institution of public education in the United States" (Sizer, 1992, p. 22). Cuban (1989) states that "the dream of making teachers more efficient (that is, of getting students to learn more in less time with less effort and at less cost) has a checkered history extending back to medieval colleges and schools" (p. 380). Currently, despite the occasional defender of the schools who views the decline in social institutions generally as having rapidly outpaced that of the schools (Bracey, 1992; Graham, 1992), or that the focus has only been on failing schools, rather than on succeeding schools (Wood, 1992), "the past several years have seen mounting evidence that the general public believes that schools are often either ineffective or at best unsatisfactory" (Rosenberger & Plimpton, 1975, p. 469).

Although increased media attention may have given calls for reform more general access to the public, and more calls speak of the "crisis" in education, the literature on reform strains credulity to some extent, if only because "we've heard it all before." A number of educators have suggested that the phenomenon of the "crisis of schooling" literature is actually cyclical in nature (Keesbury 1984; Reagan 1989; Cuban 1989). Timothy Reagan (1985) calls this the "locust theory" in which critics of public schooling periodically descend upon educators, filled with short-term wrath and indignation, and then dissipate and become forgotten as some new national crisis or fad emerges to occupy their, and the general public's, attention.

Cuban (1989) stresses that schools react and adapt to the economic and political forces embedded in these cyclical turns. In the years when conservative values stress private interests (i.e., the 1920's, 1950's, and 1980's), schools were concerned with high academic standards, orderliness, efficiency, and productivity. Reforms were therefore designed to deal with problems of inferior academic quality, lack of discipline in schools, and inefficiencies in operating schools. In years when liberal values dominated (i.e., in the early 1900's, 1930's, and 1960's), school reforms dealt with students who were outsiders, broadening what schools do in the community, and equal treatment. Bellah, et al. (1985), refer to the "tension between self-reliant competitive enterprise and a sense of public solidarity"(p. 256). Beyer, et. al. (1989) see this tension as having originated in the "contrast between the equality, community, and participation fostered in our democratic rhetoric and the competitive, nonegalitarian, and individualistic nature of economic practices in a capitalistic society" (p. vi).

The school remains one of the most democratic institutions in American society and, as such, is a vehicle through which subordinate groups can redress particular grievances, such as social inequality and economic insecurity (Berman, 1989). Schools are not only instructional sites, but cultural and political sites that represent areas of accommodation and contestation among differentially empowered cultural and economic groups (Giroux, 1988). "In public education the social conflict is expressed in the conflict between reforms aimed at reproducing the inequalities required for social efficiency under monopoly capitalism and reform aimed at equalizing opportunities in pursuit of democratic and constitutional ideals" (Carnoy & Levin, 1985, p. 24). Popkewitz (1987) similarly sees the predicament of schools as responding to social pressures which expect schools "to intervene and correct social inequities, while at the same time contributing to the ongoing dynamics of reproduction and production in society" (p. 18). The school therefore, is pulled in conflicting directions between the poles of democracy at the one extreme and inequality at the other (Berman, 1989). Boyd (1982) believes that solutions to any performance and public support problems facing the public schools are elusive because the public desires that public schools be simultaneously efficient, equitable, and responsive to consumers.

The irony of the fact that so many citizens have given up hope for public education and allowed once marginal issues to dominate the debate, is that the public schools remain one of the relatively most accessible institutions to democratic influence (Meier, 1995, p. 79).

Martin (1989) openly criticizes Sizer, Goodlad, Boyer, and Adler among others as unrealistically supporting the dual goals of social equality and technocratic elitism. The knowledge of the inherent contradictions present in "reforms" that claim to seek both "excellence" and "equality" simultaneously through grand phrases but without specific details, should heighten useful cynicism when given reforms are presented as panaceas. Both the optimist and the pessimist can be satisfied in the knowledge that, like the weather, a given reform movement is likely to change dramatically and without much notice.

Any student of this "reform" era must also consider the fact that it is not just the schools that the public wants "reformed." We now commonly hear of and often speak of government reform, healthcare reform, and so on. Exactly when support from the public began to erode is unclear, but, according to Eisner (1992), its effects are "unmistakable," as one institution after another has lost its hold on public confidence. Raywid (1990) similarly speaks of the increasing public skepticism about major societal institutions and of the growing lack of confidence in large organizations. There is a popular perception, whether true or not, that large institutional bureaucracies (such as schools), have come to operate principally for the benefit of the staff employed by them rather than for the benefit of those for whom the service is intended (Illich, 1970; Holmes & Wynne, 1989).

Whatever the reality, Cornbleth (1989) refers to "crisis language" as an everyday part of our political and social lives. "Whatever the perceived threat to life, liberty, property, and/or happiness, typically it is seen to stem from forces beyond our immediate control but to be resolvable if we are willing to make the necessary sacrifices" (p. 10).

Larry Cuban (1989) prefaces an article on "The Persistence of Reform in American Schools" with the famous quote by H.L. Mencken, "For every complicated problem there is a solution that is short, simple, and wrong." Nothing better describes the cynicism we should feel when a given "reform" is considered. Despite numerous efforts to "reform" the schools in general and teaching in particular, classrooms seem to be pretty much the same as they had been prior to the reform efforts.

There exists school reform literature written by persons from almost all walks of life, some having backgrounds in education, some not, some seeking fine tuning, some complete overhauls, some with obvious political agendas, some with unknown agendas. The criticisms of America's public schools are many and varied, ranging from pleas for more discipline, and more "basics," to pleas for more spending, more inclusion, and more professionalization. Since "A Nation at Risk" (1983, April), the weight of the literature describes these quite different solutions as "two waves" of reform (see inter alia, Goodlad, et al., 1990, p. 224; Lieberman, 1988) .

The two contrasting "waves" of more teacher autonomy on the one hand and greater standards, regulations, and less autonomy on the other hand frame most of the reform debate. Were children not involved, the contradictions in the literature would be as amusing, as they are amazing. The first "wave" lambasted teachers for the nation's educational shortcomings; the second "wave" empowers them as the key change agents in education (Conley & Cooper, 1991). Petrie (1990) asserts that the conventional wisdom concerning the two waves of reform has been that the first wave was characterized by the "imposition of top-down reforms that essentially asked teachers to do more of the same but to do it better"(p. 14), while the second wave was "characterized by a recognition of the systemic nature of the educational enterprise and the necessity of putting the teacher at the center of ... reform" (p. 14).

Sizer (1992) speaks of a third "wave" when he divides the school "remedies" into three groups: (1) the oblique strategy which seeks more accountability and increased regulation; (2) the direct strategy which assumes that schools are profoundly flawed and that reform requires fresh, sensibly designed institutions; and (3) the systemic strategy which assumes that both the oblique and direct strategies will fail and that "choice" for parents as consumers is the only method which will "overcome inertia and the hammerlock that the professional interests appear to have on public education" (pp. 22-23).

Chester Finn, a Reagan education department appointee, has said that the "shortcomings of American education arise from the maintenance of archaic practices (such as the abbreviated school year typical of an agrarian society), dysfunctional customs (such as the insistence that teachers be paid uniformly regardless of performance), and cumbersome governance arrangements (such as entrusting decisions to fifteen thousand local school boards at a time when the entire nation is imperiled) and from strongly held but mistaken ideas and beliefs (such as the view that boosting a child's self-esteem is more important than ensuring that he or she acquires intellectual skills and knowledge)" (Finn, 1991, p. xv). Whether or not Finn is correct, and despite his and the other rhetoric of our times, any sweeping reforms that would cross school districts has, for the most part, yet to be implemented.

Essentially then, the popular notion of school reform has been latched onto by a multitude of sources, with varying degrees of credibility, supporting radically different proposals based on radically different perceptions of the "problems." In other words, so much "mush." "School reform efforts ... were crippled by the absence of clear objectives and the dearth of benchmarks by which progress could be gauged" (Finn, 1991, p. 128).

Another significant obstacle in the path toward any agreement of what "good reform" might be, has been the proliferation and power of interest groups. "American education is a sprawling labyrinth in which reforms disappear. A thousand interest groups jostle and vie to maintain their status, power, and revenue flow" (Finn, p. 179). Constituencies of a school tend to agree less on common purpose and education (Ravitch, 1983). Each group concentrates on issues important to its members (First, 1992). "Rather than defend the schools against charges of destroying the economy and question the value of sweeping reforms, educational groups have tended to ask for more money and greater protection of their interests" (Spring, 1988, p. 61).

Do the reports of all the blue-ribbon commissions and expert panels make any appreciable difference? Wimpelberg and Ginsberg (1989) write: "First, commission reports seldom have much direct, sustained impact on schools and classrooms; second, they recur in perpetuum, nevertheless; and, third, commission advocates insist - in the face of apparent counter-evidence - that generic school improvement is a reasonably straightforward, specifiable, and achievable condition" (p. 13). Reagan's second education secretary William J. Bennett, as "Drug Czar" under President Bush referred to the historic education summit with the governors in 1989, as "the standard Democratic pap and Republican pap. And something that rhymes with pap...much of the discussion proceeded in a total absence of knowledge of what takes place in the schools" (First, 1992, p. 72).

Ernest Hemingway, in the early 1960's, told an interviewer that the one essential ingredient present in a great writer, was "a built-in, shockproof crap detector." In 1969, Postman & Weingartner cited Hemingway's requirement for great writing, and deemed it an appropriate consideration for schools (Postman & Weingartner, 1969, p. 3). However indelicate Hemingway's words may have been, they are worth noting when sorting through the ever growing maze of reform literature. "The truly educated person should understand how ambiguous are the goals of education, and how complex the means to be used to reach those goals" (Reich, 1989, p. 96).

In wading through the "quagmire," being always careful to detect "crap," there is the important issue of teachers' oganizations influence upon the public schools. Within that issue and underlying most of school "reform" is the debate concerning teacher competency. Given the lack of consensus about what needs reforming, and who should do the reforming, this objective look at teacher dismissal through a clearly defined framework of litigation should set this study apart from the bulk of reform literature.

Whether this trend toward "reform" seeking is appropriate or not, like most aspects and expressions of human life, school reform is more easily discussed than implemented. All habits are difficult to change, and the "habits of schooling are deep, powerful, and hard to budge" (Meier, 1992, p. 596). "No public institution is more deeply entrenched in habitual behavior than schools" (Meier, p. 596). Other researchers have made similar conclusions concerning the extremely conservative nature of schools as social institutions resistant to change (Finn, 1991; Goens & Clover, 1991; Perelman, 1987). Schools as bureaucracies, are by their nature highly resistant to change. "Bureaucracies are the repositories of conventional assumptions and standard practices - two of the greatest accelerators of entropy" (Postman & Weingartner, 1969, p. 12). Sociologists as well as those within the education profession have noted that resistance to change is not unique to schools, for all social systems develop patterns of behavior and organizational arrangements which serve to maintain the status quo (Brookover & Erickson, 1975). "Organizations enable routine or predictable behaviors to continue without a need for continuing bargaining; and in so doing, strategies and structures become institutionalized" (Jones & Maloy, 1988, p. 93). All organizations, including schools, operate in predictable ways with remarkable consistency, thereby frustrating change (Jones & Maloy, 1988). The fact that schools would resist mandated change is predicted by classical organization theory, since resistance and/or reformulation of external efforts at reform, is a natural effort to maintain boundaries (DeYoung, 1982).

Beyond such normalcy however, schools as institutions may resist change even more strongly than other segments of society having been not only resistant to reform, but apparently immune to long-term, significant change (Goens & Clover, 1991). "Despite shifts in instructional techniques and new knowledge, school organizational structures have remained remarkably the same for decades" (Jones & Maloy, 1988, p. 21).

Another consideration is the distinction between changing policy and changing practice. Policy is easier to change than practice (Eisner, 1992). Berman (1989) suggests that the history of public education clearly shows a strong resistance to structural change, although "curricular adaptation" (p. 62) in response to externally generated demands of the society is less resisted. Giroux (1988), among others, expresses his disbelief at the thinking on the part of some reformers that if the curriculum were changed, the school's "problems" would be "fixed."

If we accept, either from the research or from our own life experiences, that changing is more difficult than not changing, then we are equipped with the knowledge that reform will be difficult to implement. Given the difficulty of changing habits, reform proposals that fail to consider the entrenched "interests" within and outside our schools, are doomed to fail.

Whether "reform" fails or succeeds will, in large part, be dependant upon the public's willingness to change. Since reform means change, there is necessarily the implication in the continually growing dearth of "reform" literature, that the present "unreformed" system is at worst a failure, or at best less than it could be. Richard Elmore (1990) speaks in terms even more broad than "school reform," when he proposes "school restructuring." Elmore believes that there is a "fragile consensus that public schools, as they are presently constituted, are not capable of meeting society's expectations for the education of young people"(p. 1). Raywid (1990) speaks of the restructuring required as "nothing short of fundamental change affecting the practices of everyone within a school" (p. 152).

In contrast, Cuban (1989, p. 374), defines school reform as "a planned solution to a perceived problem." School reforms are political solutions to specific problems defined by a given group at a given time. The ability to achieve consensus is as dependent upon the time and place and context of a proposal as it is upon the quality of a proposal.

Patricia A. Graham (1992) acknowledges that there is a need to improve many of our schools, but she believes that fundamental changes in attitude and action by many segments of society are required if education is to improve. "Unless Americans as a people come to value both their children and their children's educations more than they currently do, efforts to improve schools alone will be but a finger in the dike against the flood of domestic malaise"(p. 8).

Evidence of the difficulty in enacting sweeping reforms, and of the difficulty of consensus, is provided by the abundance of "school reform" literature. Much of the literature comes from the 1960's when, in the minds of the public generally, and educational commentators specifically, the greatest concern about and "need" for reform began. The 1960's were also the period in which the public labor movement began to show the militancy that the private sector had shown decades earlier (Gee, 1979). It is from these beginnings, that over 30 years of reform literature and teacher union and collective bargaining literature arose and have provided us with our present knowledge level of these complex and interrelated concepts. As of this writing, the 1990's are still a period in which much is written about reform, but little is actually reformed.

Proposals at the state and district levels attempt reform by such measures as strengthening graduation requirements and lengthening the school day and year. The assumption underlying most vague "school reform" proposals is that changing the structure will automatically solve the substantive problems or that structural overhaul is prerequisite to their solution (Bergen, 1992). Any assumptions about school reform, however, need to be understood in the larger context of society. There exist deep philosophical differences about the "solutions," for our schools "problems" and probably more importantly, there exist deep philosophical differences about what the "problems" are (e.g., Boyer, 1983; Goodlad, 1984; Sizer, 1984; Cuban, 1989). Whether or not the problems are as deep as some believe, and whether or not the problems and/or solutions may ever allow for a consensus, the fact that the need for reform is so prevalent in the literature, the media, and the public at large, presents ample reason to study schools in a form that can produce hard data.

Schools Cannot, by Themselves, "Reform" Society

Many Americans would prefer that the discussion of the problems of education be limited to the "failures of schools." However appealing that is to those outside of schools, who then are spared the burden of correcting the problems, it is wrong both analytically and politically (Graham, 1992). There have been attempts to find a simple solution, but we must finally come to the conclusion that our society must strengthen its commitment to education, and that the schools by themselves cannot bring about improved education for everybody (Graham, 1992; Goodwin, 1992).

The belief that schools have an important impact on children is not usually open to debate. Likewise, the importance of "good" teaching is also assumed, particularly in cases where children's home environments devalue them (Kidder, 1990). Accepting that, many researchers have concluded that school is not the most important influence in children's progress (Rutter, et al., 1979; Coleman, et al., 1966). The young person who diligently attends class six hours a day, 180 days a year, from kindergarten through twelfth grade, will, at the age of eighteen, have spent just 9 percent of her hours of life in school (Finn, 1991). Bernstein (1970) concluded that education cannot compensate for the inequities of society. Coleman, et al., (1966) likewise concluded that social and economic factors outweigh any effects of schools and teachers.

Brookover & Erickson (1975) conclude that for the school to change the social structure implies considerable change in the economic system, the political system, and every other system including help from the students and their families. There is a "constant reciprocal interaction and influence"(Brookover & Erickson, p. 118) among the institutions within the society, so that changes in one system are dependant upon changes within the others. Whether change is needed from teachers or from the actual institutions of schools, to expect any group to change, without changing the environment and institutions around them may be unrealistic. "Teaching can be changed only by reinventing the institutions within which teaching takes place" (Meier, 1992, p. 600). "Groups influence education within a complex system that is influenced by multiple variables. Power, leadership resources, political structure, personal interests, control of governance, and other circumstances are additionally important variables influencing the nature of schooling" (Kimbrough, 1982, p. 27). Since school reforms are adaptations to larger social, economic, and political issues within the nation (Cuban, 1989), "when the nation trips, schools take the fall" (p. 386).

In a pamphlet published by the U.S. Department of Education in 1986, What Works: Research About Teaching and Learning, traditional conventional wisdom about schools received substantial confirmation. This publication provides a synthesis on good educational practice which supports the views that teachers have commonly held: that parents must provide a good head start and continuous support in order for children to succeed in school (Dobay, 1988).

Just as there are no two schools and no two children with the same circumstances, there is no single combination of variables that can be used to improve the effectiveness of every school (Brookover, et al., 1979). Put another way, there is no simple recipe or easy-to-assemble model (Purkey & Smith, 1983; Davis & Thomas, 1989) that is appropriate for every situation. Such awareness does not suggest that we collectively throw up our hands and walk away, but rather points up the importance of schooling, beyond information distribution to its importance as a setting for teaching and learning, and in the messages it delivers as a social organization.

The Role of Teachers in "Reform"

There is no consensus about what reform should be implemented, and similarly, there is no consensus about the part that teachers should play in any reform, even though any sweeping reform that might be attempted would, necessarily, greatly impact teachers. Traditionally, teachers have not participated in the adoption of major reforms because of their limited access to strategic decision making (Firestone & Bader, 1992). Many believe, however, that "there can be no significant innovation in education that does not have at its center the attitudes of teachers, and it is an illusion to think otherwise" (Postman & Weingartner, 1969, p. 33).

Criticism about the effectiveness of teachers has come from a variety of sources, see (Adler, 1992, Bennett, 1988, Bloom, 1987, Sykes, 1984, and Goodlad, 1988 & 1990). All sides call for teachers to do "better" work on behalf of our children, and it has been understandably difficult for teachers not to feel defensive or defeated when others far from the daily life of a classroom call for school reform

(Clifford & Friesen, 1993).

　　Much of the school reform literature, which almost universally laments the condition of our schools, invokes the importance of teachers, lays more demands for accountability on them -- and then leaves them out of the process (Goodlad, 1990; Conley & Cooper, 1991). Sarason (1971) perhaps said it best "the modal process of change in schools is one which insults the intelligence of teachers by expecting them to install programs about which they have not been consulted and which they have had no hand in developing or usually much say in modifying" (see also Grant, 1993). The exclusion of teachers and administrators in most educational reform discussion is "deplorable" (Gross, 1988, p. 108). If "deplorable" might seem a bit strong, it is at least naive to suggest, as have political reformers, organizational leaders, and technical experts, that the occasional presence of one teacher on a blue-ribbon panel alters this pattern of exclusion (Cooper, 1988). In fact, many "reformers" who harshly criticize teachers expect them to transform their practice either by themselves or under pressure from laypersons lacking professional knowledge and skill (Katz, 1992).

　　To complicate school reform even more, not everyone agrees that teachers should be at the heart of reform, some "reformers" feel that change must come from outside the schools. "Any promise of change from within is an illusion" (Gatto, et al., 1993, p. 83). This school of thought focuses upon "choice" as a means of instilling competition, and while not directly blaming teachers for the "problems" within schools, there is the overriding belief that schools are too badly broken to fix, absent some sort of radical outside reform.

　　If any reform of the public schools is contemplated, teachers would logically seem to be at the starting point. In past public discussions of educational goals and practices, however, teachers tend not to be thought of as authors of reform, but more likely as part of the problem (Warren, 1989). This study proposes an approach that focuses upon teachers as the hope for solid and productive reform, not as an obstacle on the path to reform. A concentration on advancing an agenda of what schools ought to be (Bracey, 1992). The road to improving teaching and learning requires reformers to understand the culture of teaching and to work with teachers in reforming schools (Conley & Cooper, 1991). Farrar (1990) points out, what should be obvious to reformers, that whatever policymakers decide, the "front line of education -- teachers and administrators -- will be involved one way or another in decisions about what to do to improve the schools" (p. 11).

Chapter 6

The Vague Concept of "Professionalism"

This chapter considers the concept of "professionalism," including the definitions of professionalism, and the context of professionalism as used in this study with emphasis upon professionalism in teaching. The impact of unionism upon professionalism and the impact of professionalism upon unionism will also be discussed. Ultimately, distinctions between unionism and professionalism will be considered. Related topics such as teacher licensing, tenure, teacher malpractice considerations, and professional relationships will also be addressed as the literature has commonly addressed them.

Most teachers and academics, at least according to the majority of the professionalism literature, tend to wholeheartedly support "professionalism" for teachers. What exactly constitutes professionalism, however, tends not to be so easily agreed upon. Within that broad context in which it is difficult to agree upon what the concept of "professionalism" means, lies the even greater difficulty of defining what "teaching" means. Added to that already complex mix are attempts to define the role of teacher "unions" or teacher "professional associations." Most of the recent research on teaching suggests that the value of unions for teachers is difficult to ascertain because of the "complexity and diversity of what teachers do, how they think about what they do, and the contexts in which they work" (Bascia, 1994, p. 6).

Most of the literature written tends to discuss the apparently self-evident principle that teachers should be thoroughly schooled and helpfully inducted, autonomous, responsible, valued professionals (See Devaney & Sykes, 1988, p. 3). One of the significant "reforms" of the 1980's has been the view that teaching will be more effective if teachers are treated as professionals (Strike & Ternasky, 1993). It is not difficult to find a majority of teachers who support professional-level salaries, benefits, and perquisites; but support for professional-level responsibility for decisions and professional-level adherence to standards of practice is more difficult to obtain (Devaney & Sykes, p. 3).

The ideology of professionalism needs to be placed within the context of the historical development of the division of labor, and the dynamics of social class, race, ethnicity, and gender that shaped the history of schools in general, and teaching in particular (Beyer, 1992). To understand teaching as a presumed profession, we must understand the context of other social and institutional forces that have created today's view of teachers, both among teachers themselves and the public at large. The professionalization of teaching took much of its support from the prevailing attitudes, institutions, and social dynamics present throughout society (Beyer, p. 138). Teaching has never been a high-status occupation in the United States. Willard Waller, in his 1932 study of teacher status, The Sociology of Teaching, noted that "the teacher in our culture has always been among the persons of little importance" (Toch, 1991, p. 136).

"The role played by the feminization of teaching upon the profession of teaching"

Michael Apple (1987) wrote that "any attempt at fully understanding teaching...needs to situate...current tendencies into the considerably longer history of which they are a part" (p. 57). Since the mid 1800's, teaching has been largely a female occupation. In a society which was permeated with sexist conventions about success, the identification of teaching with women often meant that teachers were held in low esteem (Rury, 1989). The association of teaching with women at a time when virtually all other professions in America were dominated by men, helped to assure that teaching would not be recognized as a profession in the same terms as law or medicine (Rury,

p. 10). Susan B. Anthony in her 1881 address to the NEA convention, clearly stated her impression of the status problem of teaching: "Do you not see that as long as society says that a woman is incompetent to be a lawyer, a minister, or a doctor; but has ample ability to be a teacher, every male who chooses the teaching profession acknowledges that he has no more brains than a woman?" (Herndon, 1983, p. 68; Fraser, 1989, p. 122). The perceptions were unmistakeable then as now, that if the "best students," male or female, do not choose teaching, but instead choose law, medicine, theology, or some other "science," then teaching will not be afforded the same societal "status." The unequal opportunities afforded white men in fields such as medicine, law, science, business, and the ministry, greatly affected the gender specificity of the teaching force (Beyer, 1992).

It is no coincidence that the rise of teacher's organizations came with the rise of suffrage. Teachers recognized that education was a political football in mayoral contests. Their inability to vote had negative effects on their ability to negotiate (Murphy, 1990). There is some basis for the "feminization factor" having slowed the "professionalization" of teaching, just as other female dominated careers have similarly been slowed in their path toward greater influence and prestige. The fact that male dominated higher education has greater autonomy, prestige, status, and legitimacy, leads reasonably to the conclusion that as in society at large, our history suggests that discrimination against women has impacted the professionalization of education. Whether the ability to negotiate was important to improve education generally in relation to other public expenditures, or specifically to improve teacher salaries, tended to depend upon which side of the fence you were on. Women schoolteachers stood at the boundaries between professionalism and unionism as they assessed the two movements that dominated educational discourse (Murphy, p. 47).

The fact that more cases exist concerning teacher dismissals in recent years, is probably less attributible to having more men in the profession, than in the increase throughout society of more litigation. However, the apparent willingness of men to challenge their dismissals more readily than women have historically, might indicate more about our society and our legal system, than a mere change in demographics. If our courts have been guilty of gender bias, then it should come as no surprise that many women teachers dismissed by predominantly male school boards have been reluctant to expect any better treatment of their grievances in male dominated courts.

Implications of School Reform on "Professionalism"

The impact the "excellence" movement had, and is having upon teachers is an appropriate starting point for a study of the "professionalism" of teachers. A common theme throughout two major reports on teaching and teacher education done in 1986, conclude that teaching in America's public schools will not improve and live up to the nation's demands until classroom teachers see themselves, and come to be accepted by the public, as professionals (See Tomorrow's Teachers: A Report of the Holmes Group, and A Nation Prepared: Teachers for the Twenty-first Century, the recommendations of the Carnegie Forum on Education and the Economy's Task Force on Teaching as a Profession; Herbst, 1989, p. 213). That these two documents direct their concern and effort toward the professionalization of teaching, is not disputed. What is disputed is whether the view of professionalization expressed in the documents has much in common with the realities of teaching today (Beyer et al., 1989).

A recurrent theme throughout this study is that what exactly is meant by "professionals" is highly subjective and context controlled, but generally these major reports are referring to "professionals" as persons having a greater degree of autonomy and who will exhibit and be subject to both internal and external "professional" standards of conduct and performance. Albert Shanker (1989) reinforces the "need for professional autonomy " in his view that prospective teachers must be assured that "they will not be treated like factory hands, strictly supervised at every point in the working day and robbed of every opportunity of exercising their own judgment" (p. 106).

Like many other reports, the Carnegie and Holmes proposals assume that we know what we mean and are all agreed on what improved teaching and improved education would be like (Beyer et al., 1989). Like the "excellence" movement, these reports reduce student learning to numerical data as assessed by some sort of standardized perfomance measure.

In today's school reform debate then, there exist two very different theories or "waves" as to how to best "reform" our schools. One theory involves national testing proposals, and is advocated by such luminaries as former President Bush in his America 2000 proposal.

This school of reform would improve education by developing more tests and tying federal funds to schools' test scores (Darling-Hammond, 1992). This theory's reliance upon "authentic assessment" requires changes among teachers as a group. America 2000 is not significantly different from the proliferation of laws in the 1970's that sought to prescribe not only school inputs, but school procedures and even student outcomes. The buzzwords of the 1970's were "back to the basics" and "accountability," reflecting the view that schools had accommodated too many frills and left unchecked, would forget or shirk their basic mission (Darling-Hammond, 1988).   A second theory attends more to the qualifications and capacities of teachers and to developing schools as inquiring, collaborative organizations than to changes in programs, curricula, and management systems (Darling-Hammond, 1992, p. 22). The talk has been of "professionalizing" teaching and "restructuring" schools (Lieberman, Saxl, Miles, 1988, p. 148).

As these two schools of thought pull in contrasting directions, the issue of "professionalism" in teaching appears to rest its hopes squarely on the success of the second theory, and the consequent failure of the first. Berry & Ginsberg (1991) put it quite succintly "for teacher professionalism to occur, many first wave policy reforms must be significantly altered or abandoned" (p. 148). Advocates of the second theory, base their arguments on the professional competence of educators to determine what is appropriate for the educational program (Brookover & Erickson, 1975). Beyond "mere" competence, inherent in any proposals to change the way schools operate is the need for the allowance of teachers to have time for "professional development" (Nystrand, 1992, p. 26).

Regardless of the success or the merits of either "wave" of reform, the marked contrast between the two positions provides fertile ground for "organizational politics" and debate, but barren ground for real "reform." "Organizational politics" is defined as "the contest that occurs over various possible logics of action and their various manifestations" (Bacharach & Mundell, 1993, p. 428). Whether manifest as ideologies, policies, goals, or means, the struggle over logics of action is the focus of the symbolic and real political contests within organizations (Bacharach & Mundell, p. 430). This struggle, whether real or symbolic, is indicative of the lack of consensus within the school reform literature, which frames the political debate concerning "school reform."

The dilemma for school reform lies in the fact that we have developed a system of schooling that relies on externally developed policies and mandates to assure public accountability, which requires teachers to follow "standard operating procedures." Consequently, teachers cannot properly be held professionally accountable; only accountable for following "standard operating procedures" (Darling-Hammond, 1988, p. 60). In accordance with the belief that simply following orders absolves the actor of blame, some critics of public education blame the "system" while absolving the teachers (Dobay, 1988). "Misinformed Americans hold teachers responsible for the plight of public education. Yet teachers exercise little real influence over policies affecting their work" (Dobay, p. 28).

While some of the new reformers recognize that public education has become overregulated and that the teaching occupation has become unattractive to many talented students, their reform proposals urge still greater involvement of policy makers in shaping schools (Darling-Hammond, 1988). Consequently, we see states passing laws that pay lip service to teacher professionalism while, simultaneously, requiring greater restraints on curricula, textbooks, tests, and teaching methods (Darling-Hammond, 1987).

Changes in teacher education, more time for professional development, and decentralization of the decision-making process in the schools are many of the goals of teachers in support of the second theory. It is teachers, through their organizations who seem to be attempting to persuade school administrations in particular, and society at large, that greater professionalization of the "workers" within the schools will achieve greater motivation, responsiveness, and judgment, all of which will benefit the students and thereby society. It is within this framework of reform that any study of "professionalism" in education rests.

"Professionalism" as a Means to School Reform

Ginsburg (1987) refers to the "proverbial question: is teaching a profession?"(p. 86). He then goes on to say that "too much has already been written on this question"(p. 86). Firestone and Bader (1992) similarly assert that most of the rhetoric on teacher reform concerns professionalism. This study addresses the professionalism literature because of its importance to the teaching "profession," the "reform" of the schools, and ultimately the effect of the various "reforms" upon the realities of teaching. Ignoring "professionalism" within the reform literature and within the rhetoric of the AFT and NEA themselves, would do a disservice to any study in which collective bargaining and teacher unionism are central players. At the same time, like Ginsburg, this study places little value upon any "answer" that might solve the proverbial question.   "The fact that there are contradictory aspects of the ideology of professionalism makes it more worthy of study, as a way to encourage reflection about other contradictions in society" (Ginsburg, 1987, p. 120).

"Questions of professionalization and professionalism seem to arise when two conditions obtain: when practitioners in the field in which those questions are being debated find themselves under external attack, and when those practitioners are themselves suffering anxiety about their own membership in a coherent, identifiable community" (Beyer, et al., 1989, p. 90-91). Both conditions seem to be present within the education reform literature today.

The academic literature and indeed, the lay literature concerning "professionalism" is vast and hardly conclusive. The inconclusiveness stems from the fact that no reasonable "final" definition can be satisfactory for all situations at all times. "The notions of profession, professionalism, and professionalization are social constructs and can 'mean' only what a group of people in a given culture at a given time might want them to mean" (Soder, 1990, p. 44). Specifically, "professionalism" as a socially constructed concept, is dependent entirely upon society's acceptance or lack of acceptance of any given profession. In American society, professionalism is a concept that is usually applied in a morally evaluative manner-that is, one occupational group is better (e.g., medicine) than another (e.g., teaching)(Berry & Ginsberg, 1991). Becker (1962, p. 33) suggests that a profession is nothing more than an "occupation which has been fortunate enough in the politics of today's work world to gain and maintain possession of that honorific title." A profession develops its status, in part, by its arcane knowledge which cannot be applied routinely and, in part, by the knowledge base which defines the nature of the profession itself (Berry & Ginsberg, 1991). Densmore (1987) defines professionalism as an "ideal to which individuals and occupational groups aspire that distinguishes them from other workers" (p. 135). However, this aspiration obscures actual job functions, work practices, and social relations (Densmore, 1987). While the aspiration to be "professional" is harmless in itself, in the case of teaching, some scholars (Densmore, 1987; Larson, 1977), believe that the concern with status and privileges vis-a-vis other employees, obscures teacher-professionals' actual lack of power, their subordination, and their commonalities with other workers.

Societal norms have granted teaching low status, and a lack of respect. As a result of such status, teachers have little voice in setting or influencing public policies that affect them professionally. The "shadowed social standing" (Lortie, 1975, p. 10) of teachers allows politicians and administrators to dominate education, while the voices of teachers are silent (Goodwin, 1987, p. 32). The dilemma for teachers is apparent, as public servants they are damned if they complain about the conditions of their work, and they are derided and/or ignored if they merely accept their fate without complaint.

The potential conflict between teacher autonomy and the tradition of democratic control over education is at the heart of the professionalization debate. "Control over professional activity by professionals" or "those who know should rule," conflicts with our democratic ideals and the input sought from school boards, parents, communities, and from the students themselves (Strike, 1990, p. 203). In the "established" legal profession, lawyers define meaning and substance of justice while in the medical profession doctors define the meaning and substance of health (Darling-Hammond, 1985). In contrast, teachers do not define the nature of education (Berry & Ginsberg, 1991). "The central issue in teacher professionalization is autonomy in all its guises" (Macmillan, 1993). In the context of teaching, "professionalism is best understood as an ideological response to degraded work conditions" (Densmore, 1987, p. 140).

"Professionalism" as a Status

Mostly due to the preoccupation with status that has seemingly consumed much of the "professionalism" literature, the focus was and is, upon somehow increasing the outside perceptions of the teaching "profession." A concern with professionalism is intended to raise the status and rewards of teaching, attract more able and intelligent people to the field, and allow teachers greater control over the content and the conduct of their work (Ayers, 1992). This focus is also beset with problems, for if teachers see professionalism as a type of elitism separating them from the community at large, a successful "partnership" among teachers, parents, administrators, and the community will be more difficult (Ayers, 1992). Professionalism, could also lead to an overemphasis on developing a "knowledge base" for teaching and a corresponding weakening of attributes like "compassion"(p. 24).

What does "professional" mean when applied to teachers? Formally, it means a member of an occupation with recognized professional status (Brandt, 1993, p. 5). Amy Gutmann (1987, p. 77), identifies four rewards of professionalism -- the pleasures of performance, high salary, status, and the exercise of authority over other people. Andrew Abbott (1988, p. 8), defines a profession as "an exclusive occupational group applying somewhat abstract knowledge to particular cases." Knowledge may be the fact that distinguishes professionals from other workers. Raelin (1986, p. 47), defines a profession as an "occupation requiring expert knowledge that justifies a monopoly of services granted by government licensing." Using that definition, teachers would be professionals even without controlling entrance to the field, teaching practices, salaries, or working conditions (Goens & Clover, 1991). Educators have desired to be recognized as professionals for generations, but the current drive for professionalization originated in the mid-1980's, when it became apparent to policymakers that mandates by themselves were not going to bring substantially higher achievement.

The literature on "professionalism" consists of three schools of thought: The first is that a distinctive set of traits defined the professions as a coherent set of occupations. Although no consensus existed about the precise set of characteristics defining professions, many analysts concentrated on the combination of expertise, collective organization and collegial control, ethical standards, and work in a "public service" (Brint, 1993). The second school of thought is that there can be no universal set of traits, and rather the "process" of professionalization was the central force, not the concept of professions (Brint, p. 261). The third school of thought also denied any universality, and focused on the historical and contemporary usage of the term by various interested parties.

Although teachers' pleas for greater professionalization may indicate that we, or even they, do not know for certain what "professional conduct" is, the courts have heard cases alleging "unprofessional conduct" Roberts v. Santa Cruz, 778 P.2d 1294. 55 Ed. Law Rptr. 1175, (Ariz. App. 1989). It would seem to be a logical extension then, that if a teacher can be punished for "unprofessional conduct," that same teacher must be assumed to be acting "professionally" in the ordinary course of his/her teaching duties.

In 1986, two groups published major reports converging on professionalizing teaching as a solution to some of the criticisms of schooling. The Carnegie Task Force on Teaching as a Profession, and the Holmes Group's "Tomorrow's Teachers" both argued that the quality of public education can only be improved if teaching is turned into a full-fledged profession (Larabee, 1992, p. 124; Soder, 1990, p. 37). In the "pursuit of excellence" through education, "the key to success lies in creating a profession equal to the task -- a profession of well-educated teachers prepared to assume new powers and responsibilities to redesign schools for the future" (Carnegie Task Force on Teaching, 1986, p. 2). The Holmes Group (1986, p. 63) described professions as follows: "the established professions have, over time, developed a body of specialized knowledge, codified and transmitted through professional education and clinical practice." Hallmarks of a profession include mastery of a body of knowledge and skills that laypeople do not possess, autonomy in practice, and autonomy in setting standards for the field (Wise & Leibbrand, 1993). Like these prestigious consortiums, teachers' associations, particularly by the mid 1980's began publicly stating their belief that education could only improve if teaching became a true profession (Murray, 1992). The quality of instruction depended bottom-line on the quality of teachers. Unfortunately, many see inherent contradictions between teacher professionalism and membership in strong state and national unions (Hawkins, 1985, p. 41). Gary Sykes (1989) asserts that "the union posture is ill-fitted to the pursuit of professionalism" (p. 264). The operating style, underlying assumptions, strategies employed, and the issues agenda, are quite different for professionals than for unions (Sykes, 1989). The difficulty in strong unions pressing for "professionalism" is clear, as are the differences between professionals' desire for autonomy and unions desire for highly specified rules and clearly written contracts setting forth the "workers" responsibilities.

The two prongs of the teacher-professionalization effort were and are restructuring both the professional education and the work roles of teachers. These two prongs point to two key elements at the core of what we generally mean by a "profession." These two key elements are formal knowledge and workplace autonomy (Labaree, 1992). The occupational group must establish that it has mastery of a formal body of knowledge that is not accessible to the layperson and that it gives it special competence in carrying out a form of work (Labaree, p. 125). Freidson (1986) similarly included the two key elements in "one minimal characteristic," of a professional employee, "technical autonomy, the freedom to employ discretion in performing work in the light of personal, presumably schooled judgment that is not available to those without the same qualifications" (p. 141).

Professionalization means not only higher pay, but several other interrelated parts: high admission standards, excellent undergraduate and graduate preparation, continuing education on the job, and desirable working conditions (Labaree, p. 5). Working conditions in any profession encompass at least three aspects: compensation and rewards, social status, and work responsibilities (Presseisen, 1985). Teaching may, and should, provide rewards beyond money, but its social status and work responsibilities do not presently satisfy a large number of teachers. Any desire to separate a "profession" from its pay scale, is in our society, virtually impossible to do. "The economic realities of teaching play an important role in its nature: they undergird its social class position and the shape of careers within the occupation" (Lortie, 1975, p. 8). "The status of teachers within schools and within society at large has remained relatively stable over the years; in this respect, perhaps teaching illustrates our growing awareness of the rigidity of social rankings in general" (Lortie, p. 22). "Teachers are accorded an ambiguous respect directed toward guardians of the young" (Jones & Maloy, 1988, p. 25).

"The size of the teaching profession is also an important factor in the status it is awarded and, particularly, in the extent to which it can expect high rewards for its services. The cost of maintaining a well-qualified and highly-paid teaching profession in the context of mass...education...requires the backing of a community which is not only wealthy, but highly committed to education and willing to spend generously on the public services" (Banks, 1976, p. 163). Further evidence of the public's lack of concern for increasing teacher pay comes from most recent <u>Phi Delta Kappan/Gallup Poll of the Public's Attitudes Toward the Public Schools</u>, in which only 3 percent of the poll's respondents cited "low pay for teachers" as one of the "biggest problems" with which the public schools must deal (Elam, Rose, Gallup, 1993, p. 139).

The past efforts of teachers and their associations to bring

higher pay to teachers as a first step has not been tremendously successful. The effort to make good teaching "scientific" rather than "artful," was an effort to increase status and pay (Dobay, 1988). Like medical doctors who gained prestige as the medical profession became more complex with the attainment of new knowledge, teachers were supposed to see increased status when the education field became more complex and more research into understanding teaching was performed (Dobay, 1988). Kultgen (1988) put forth the view that education could be seen as the paradigm for all professionals, since professional practice is always an educational process. Unfortunately for teachers, the public has not bought it. Whether teaching is as complex as lawyering or doctoring is not the issue, the issue is that the public has not bought it. Kultgen (1988) recognized that his "paradigm" argument would not carry the day with the public, who "sensing the debasement of the professional ideal in this form of pedagogy, meet the clamor of teachers for professional identity with polite skepticism"
(p. 310).

A profession consists of individuals with specialized knowledge obtained through intensive education which allows them to provide esoteric services in a near monopoly fashion to a public which recognizes and accepts the utility of the monopoly (Mayhew, 1971, p.1).

"Professionalism is an ethical code, a social bond, a pattern of mutual regulation and self-discipline" (Walzer, 1983, p. 155). In 1948, the National Labor Relations Act defined a professional as one "engaged in work predominantly intellectual....involving the consistent exercise of discretion and judgment ...of such character that the output produced cannot be standardized...and requiring knowledge of an advanced type in a field of science or learning customarily acquired by a prolonged course of specialized intellectual instruction and study" (Denemark, 1985, p. 46). The "requirement" of a base of "specialized knowledge," is problematic for some scholars, who view teaching as more art than science. The "diffuseness" of the teaching role, wherein there is not a definable expertise involving an objective body of knowledge, also impedes teaching from attaining true professional status (Banks, 1976, p. 164). The vague goals of teaching (such as individualize and teach everyone in the class) along with the ambiguous connection between what is taught and what is learned, require artistry, as opposed to scientific thought (Lieberman & Miller, 1978, p. 56). Social and organizational differences in teachers' work may lead to substantively different instructional goals, practices, and professional standards (McLaughlin & Talbert, 1993). Other researchers believe that teaching is not viewed as a profession because the complexity of teaching is hidden beneath the apparent simplicity of its execution and because it is not cloaked in unfamiliar language (Goens & Clover, 1991; Bacharach & Conley, 1989).

As early as 1956, and probably before, the professional status of teaching was doubted (Lieberman, 1956). In comparing teaching to other professions, Lieberman concluded that unlike other professionals, teachers lacked control over entry into their ranks, they were subjected to policies over which they exercised little control, they suffered high turnover rates and a low public image, and were generally dominated and overshadowed by administrators.

The definition of a "profession" is, like any profession itself, rather imprecise. Among the problems with attempting to give precision to a social or occupational role that varies as a function of the setting in which it is performed, is the fact that the role continually evolves, and is perceived differently by different segments of society (Schein, 1972, p. 8). Most, if not all persons who have studied "professions" have agreed on the necessity to use multiple criterion in order to establish a workable definition of a professional. Edgar H. Schein, in his work entitled Professional Education, included a ten-part multiple criterion definition derived from an analysis of the writings of a number of sociologists who have studied the professions, (e.g., Goode, 1957; Blau & Scott, 1962; Barber, 1963; Hughes, 1963; Gilb, 1966; Abrahamson, 1967; Parsons, 1968; Gross, 1969; Moore, 1970; Wilensky, 1964). The criteria listed tend to best fit the "ancient" professions of law, medicine, and divinity, while fitting in various degrees professions like architecture, social work, engineering, teaching, and management (Schein, 1972, p. 9). Although there is agreement with Schein as far as the multiple criteria, such as the requirements of high skill and intellectual effort and extensive formal education, other scholars have added the "tradition of group dignity" and "the involvement primarily of the exchange of service or advice in return for a fee or salary, rather than the sale of goods for profit" (Havighurst & Neugarten 1975, p. 461). Interestingly, Havighurst & Neugarten go further and state that "there can be little question that public school teaching is a profession" (Havighurst & Neugarten, p. 461). As always, the criteria that are applied to determine a profession, necessarily determines whether any given occupation may or may not be a profession. Consequently, whether teaching is a profession or not depends upon not only who you ask, but upon what criteria you apply. Holmes and Wynne (1989, p. 136), put the "value" of a common definition in perspective, when they contend that "definitions are often developed to capture the notion we already believe."

Definitions of "professional" practice commonly agree that professionals develop a specialized knowledge base from which appropriate decisions can be made on behalf of clients; that professionals have the ability to apply that knowledge in individual, non-routine circumstances; and that they have a strong ethical commitment to do what is best for the client. Questions about the scope of the autonomy that a professional has in exercising his/her qualified discretionary judgment, or about the propriety of practices within that scope, are decided by the profession itself as a group, not by clients, supervisors, or employers outside the profession (Beyer, et al., 1989). In addition, professionals usually work together to determine the requirements of credentialing and licensing (Wasley, 1991). Currently, it is difficult to describe teaching using these "professional" requirements (Wasley, p. 16). The circumstances of lack of authority and stability, of sensible working conditions and adequate compensation all add up to a denial of truly professional consideration (Herbst, 1989).

Flexner (1915), was probably the first to study and define "professionalism." A significant criticism of the present literature, is the lack of progress that has been made toward any consensus, and consequently any improvement upon Flexnor's 1915 work. Because usage varies substantively, logically, and conceptually (Freidson, 1977), some analysts have given the impression of condemning the very practice of seeking a definition. Freidson (1986), states that "profession" must be used in a specific historical and national sense. It is not a scientific concept generalizable to a wide variety of settings. "What a profession is then, is not determined solely by any single group, neither by members of an occupation, nor by those of other occupations they deal with in the course of their work... there is no way of resolving the problem of defining profession that is not arbitrary" (p. 36).

Jurgen Herbst, in <u>And Sadly Teach</u>, defines a professional as "deriving status from the education they receive and the individual and collective autonomy they claim and enjoy in the exercise of their professional duties. Within the confines of a given task, professionals decide for themselves how to proceed. They work without supervision and carry full personal responsibility for the results. They are guided by a code of ethics and are accountable for observing its commands to their professional colleagues" (Herbst, 1989). Freidson (1986) acknowledges that the "conspicuous" professions like law and medicine do have both local and state committees designated to hear complaints from consumers or colleagues and very occasionally undertake sanctions against individual members. "By and large, however, professional associations tend more to provide services to their members than to exercise control over their ethical or technical work behavior" (Freidson, 1986, p. 187).

Hughes (1963) viewed professionalism as consisting of two concepts: license and mandate. Dingwall (1983) interpreted Hughes' concepts as a license to carry out certain activities different from others, and a mandate to define, for themselves and others, proper conduct in relation to their work. The words used by Hughes, Dingwall, and Herbst differ, but their requirements for professionalism are the same.

Freidson (1986) described teaching as not a strong profession, partly because the work it does revolves around conspicuous issues that are of widespread public concern. Furthermore, education is subject to "cyclical waves of public alarm" (Freidson, p. 224). As the literature on school reform illustrates, a wide range of persons occasionally consider themselves experts on educational policy and the proper way to administer schools, allocate resources, and define public problems and needs.

Schein, among others, specifically lists teaching as a profession. Others who have studied the issue of professionalism have tended to narrow the term to include only law, medicine, and divinity. Lewis Mayhew refers to professions as "older," and "emerging." Law, medicine, and divinity fall into the former group, while teaching falls into those seen as "emerging" (Mayhew, 1971, p.1). Herbst (1989) states that "teacher professionalism does not exist everywhere within our public schools"(p. 7). As for the definition given above by Herbst, and the multiple-criterion definition preferred by many sociologists, neither apply to teachers.

Teaching is professionalized in the sense that it clearly involves a body of expert knowledge and skills learned over a period of time, it implies a set of ethics or standards of professional practice, and it attempts to maintain its profession's autonomy. However, the fact that most teachers work for large organizations rather than small professional offices makes it unclear precisely who their client is, erodes their autonomy, and weakens colleague authority in favor of line authority within the employing organization (Schein, 1972, p. 11). Freidson (1986) agrees when referring to schoolteaching as a very large practitioner group that operates within broadly defined bureaucratic constraints.

The prevailing professional norms of peer regulation and individual autonomy were, and are, in stark contrast to the subservient role of teachers in many schools (Cresswell, 1976). Undermining professional authority and integrity is the structural relationship between teachers and administrators (Hawkins, 1985). The major professions of medicine and law have professionals leading the organization and defining and producing the product. Those responsible for administering the organization are usually paid less than the professionals and exercise little actual authority, in direct contrast to teaching. (Hawkins, p. 41).

Whatever else may go along with professional status, the function of a professional is responsibility. Responsibility calls for training and judgment. The special competence often demanded of the professional is a measure of society's dependence upon the professional (Mayhew, 1971). Freidson (1986) describes professional employees as possessing technical autonomy or the right to use discretion and judgment in the performance of their work. Yet a teacher's world is governed by someone else's rules. We can hardly expect teachers to exercise judgment or to take responsiblity for the result when they have little power to shape their work (Murphy, 1993). Rather than connoting a high level of training and knowledge applied to practice that must, above all else, serve the needs of clients, many policy makers and administrators use the term "professionalism" to mean unquestioning compliance with directives. The "professional" teacher in common usage is one who does things right, rather than one who does the right things (Darling-Hammond, 1988, p. 61).

If teaching is a profession, it must have a set of standards by which teachers can be judged better and worse (Gutmann, 1987). Most of the structures within which teachers teach do not allow for more than very minimal individual recognition. One criticism of collective bargaining has been that in requiring schools to treat teachers similarly, "excellent" teachers are simply lumped together with "average" ones. The loss of individuality, in favor of equal treatment, diminishes the chances that certain teachers might receive the individual attention and rewards that they might deserve (Maeroff, 1988). There exists a tradeoff of better wages, working conditions, and hours, for the masses, in return for the sacrifice of individuality and potential professionalism. Unions in achieving gains for teachers financially, may have unwittingly, held many individual teachers down in their attempts to raise the level of all teachers equally. Ironically, the gains made by the unions through collective action, in conjunction with the "accountability movement" (Dobay, 1988), which targeted teachers as those most responsible for poor standards, caused good teachers to suffer along with bad ones.

The degree to which teaching is professionalized depends upon the setting in which it is practiced, and the manner in which the practitioner is controlled (Schein, p. 12). Still, most professional persons are employees, not practitioners, dealing with individual clients (Mayhew, 1971). As employees they owe their livelihood to the organization itself, not a given individual. Such a conflict can and does impact professional behavior, when the professional must carry out the will of the organization, even if it occasionally conflicts with that professional's own best judgment. Is the organization paying the professional to exercise his or her own best judgment always, or only when that judgment agrees with the organizational mission? Teachers are often told that they are professionals and have obligations and ethical responsibilities based on that professionalism, while simultaneously, they are told that they are employees and have little freedom and the status accorded "mere" employees (Walter, 1975, p. 20).

In the existing heirarchical system, teachers do not have the capability to make professional decisions in the best interest of their students. Nor have they developed their own knowledge base. Nor have teachers worked together to determine standards for credentialing or for measuring the efficacy of their work. These conditions stifle teachers' capacity to better the opportunities for student learning (Wasley, 1991). Within current governance and administrative structures, teachers are accountable for implementing curriculum and testing policies, assignment and promotion rules, and many other requirements, whether or not these treatments are appropriate in particular instances for particular students. As a consequence, teachers cannot be held professionally accountable, only accountable for following standard operating procedures (Darling-Hammond, 1988, p. 60). Externally developed policies and mandates set by state legislatures ensures democratic control of the schools, but it may also limit any discussion of "professionalizing" teaching to academic forums.

External control over schools by "unprofessional" boards of education runs counter to "professionalization" as the term is commonly used. "Professionals expect to be autonomous and self-directing, subject only to the constraints of competent knowledge and skill related to their task" (Freidson, 1986, p. 159). The issue becomes whether control over the practitioner's work should come from other practitioners, or from outside "non-members."

The meaning that we as a society have attached to teaching as a profession has changed over time. Similarly, medicine and law have also undergone transformations into much different professions now than in years past. The teaching profession was characterized by the ideology of the "true teacher," which fostered the view that teachers should be devoted to service, with little concern for personal gain (Murray, 1992, p. 513). The "service" aspect of teaching, combined with other factors, such as the relatively high percentage of women within the teaching ranks, have contributed to society's concern about teacher unionization and collective bargaining. Although, we seem to have little difficulty, as a society, with the high salaries earned by doctors, lawyers, and other "professionals," we tend to have tremendous difficulty when teachers and other "workers" collectively bargain in order to raise their pay.

In order to effectively come to grips with teachers' desire for increased pay and prestige, society must view teachers as "professionals," but professionals without great individual power to improve their lot in life. As relatively powerless professionals, the need for collective action should be apparent. Reconciling powerlessness with professionalism may be too difficult for most of us, and if "most of us" are the ones controlling where we allow our taxes to be spent, teachers' associations might be well advised to either abandon their desire for increased status, and concentrate on wages, hours, and working conditions, making no distinction between these workers and other powerless workers, or alternatively, to focus intently on increasing status, by increasing standards and other "internal" aspects of the profession. To desire both professionalism and to allow the public to perceive of teachers' associations as unions, has proven to be an ineffective way of raising teacher pay and prestige. The ineffectiveness is illustrated by the proliferation and tenacity of the literature concerning "professionalism" and the "need" for greater pay, without much significant "real world" application. Also significant is that most of the literature in these areas comes from authors "within" the education establishment while the literature from "outside" the education establishment still usually refers to teachers' organizations as unions.

Our country recently faced a debate over healthcare reform. One of the loudest cries heard from those opposing "reform" came from doctors who, as a result of their professional standing and expertise, have become quite accustomed to having their methods accepted without significant question. Not only have doctors, as professionals, been telling society what is good and right for it; they also have been allowed to set the terms of thinking about problems which fall within their domain. The fact that reform is considered by persons in government, who are not themselves members of the medical profession, is illustrative of the changing nature of the professions. Without commenting on the merits of healthcare reform, it is interesting to note the position of most physicians and the AMA: that reform in healthcare must be from within the profession, not from outside "non-professionals." Teachers might derive some satisfaction from the knowledge that one of the "real" professions is being "demystified" to some extent by government, and like teaching is beginning to be seen as "too important" to be left solely to the discretion of those limited few within the profession.

The Movement Towards "Professionalization"

However one views the professionalization movement, its ultimate importance for schools is in whether it adds or subtracts from student outcomes, and the answer to that is, like most educational questions, highly debatable. The importance of professionalization is somewhere between the extremes of usefulness only in enhancing teachers economic positions and as a broad and important influence in the complex cognitive-affective interaction between teachers and students, influencing the students' personality, intellectual development, and present and future life satisfaction (Havighurst & Neugarten, 1975, p. 469). Another as yet unsolved dilemma for teachers lies in the commonly held need to treat individual students as individuals and to allow for flexibility in teaching, within a climate mandating that teachers not stray from accepted paths. Many teachers are required to keep detailed lesson plans so that those "above"(administrators) and those "outside"(parents) need not worry about potential misinformation finding its way into Johnny's head. Less confidence could hardly be shown. Most persons admit that teaching and learning are complex experiences which defy exact formulation, yet teachers continue to be held accountable for lesson plans describing what teaching methods will be used and how students will demonstrate in verifiable ways what they have learned (Dobay, 1988).

For "professionalism" and collective bargaining to exist in relative harmony, the decisions made in the "professional" areas will have to be of the type in which most within the given educational enterprise, from teachers to administrators, will tend to agree upon. "Disagreements on specific issues are fine, but generally the conflict must not be of the type which polarizes teachers and administrators" (Perry & Wildman, 1970, p. 237). "Professional" aspects of teaching should not be subjects for collective bargaining, and thereby such aspects should be sheltered from the power and compromise inherent in bargaining, if "professionalism" is to be advanced. Further, whatever one's feelings about national teachers' organizations, it is the local union officers, or perhaps district officers who actually participate in the bargaining process (Aaron, 1988).

"The Captive Clientele"

When a person is dissatisfied with an attorney or a physician, that person is generally free to look elsewhere. They are also afforded the knowledge that the bar and medical associations are supposedly protecting the public from incompetence. Teachers, in contrast are employed by the public at large to provide what is, for most people, the only real opportunity for formal education for their children. A monopoly exists in that the employment relationship is between the public as a whole and teachers as a group. Where a monopoly exists, society depends upon controls to protect its interests (Walter, 1975). Many beneficiaries of social programs such as education have advanced the proposition that they should have more and greater impact upon the programs put forth to benefit them.

Nathan Glazer compared educators to doctors, social workers, and others as "professionals" servicing the public and subject to the wishes of their beneficiaries' more direct involvement in their own "care." He further stated, however, that some types of service "in which the claim to professionalism is so well grounded, that the degree of participation had to be limited, and the best example of this is health services" (Glazer, 1988, p. 105). Adding to the confusion, Glazer has previously stated that "the major professions are medicine and law; the minor professions are all the rest" (Glazer, 1974, p. 347; Soder, 1990, p. 47). Similarly, Etzioni (1969) described teaching as a "semi-profession." To complicate things further, it seems that even among the "professions" there are varying degrees of "professionalism."

Seron & Ferris (1995) add still more to the cloudiness surrounding the meaning of a true "profession" in their view that "an unbracketed time commitment distinguishes professions from other, especially blue-collar, occupations" (p. 41). Teachers who have great latitide within their own classrooms as to time-usage, and who perform many tasks such as grading papers and preparing for classes, at home and on weekends away from school; but who still are required to teach and "work" within pre-determined hours and at pre-determined work-sites, seem again to fit somewhere between a "true" autonomous profession and a non-autonomous "occupation."

Parents and students both demand and generally receive significant access to decision-making within the schools. That fact alone distinguishes education from more "mystified" professions such as medicine, and law. The "beneficiary" of education has a much more accepted role in the delivery of that education, than does the "beneficiary" of medical services, or legal advice.

The teacher professionalization literature suggests that when teachers advert to the "real" professions worthy of emulation, they advert almost exclusively to medicine or law (Soder, 1990, p. 54; Jarolimek, 1981). The silence in the literature and rhetoric concerning the "plain old occupations, crafts, and trades" suggests that teachers' gravitation toward only certain professions is based more upon their desire for "prestige by association," than upon a competent analysis of the attributes, efficacy, and value to society of the professions (Soder, p. 54).

"The Debate over the Professionalization of Teaching"

The proponents of "professionalization" for teaching are many, (see among others, Boyer, 1983; Darling-Hammond, 1988; Goodlad, Soder, & Sirotnik, 1990). The first requirement of that "professionalization" is the dependence of professional practice upon an intellectually respectable knowledge base (Macmillan, 1993). The second requirement is the presumed autonomy of the profession and its members, the freedom to make professional decisions without interference from nonprofessional persons or governmental bodies (Macmillan, 1993).

In contrast, the opponents of the "professionalization" of teachers, most notably Burbules and Densmore (1991), claim that such an advance would be detrimental to their students. The fact that there are two credible sides to the argument is evidence that, like the other "reforms," the move toward genuine "professionalization" is going to be slow at best.

Is Greater Professionalism Possible?

If teaching is not a profession, what might make it a profession? According to Albert Shanker, the long-time President of the AFT, we need to "really professionalize teaching by making it much tougher to get in and increasing the rewards" (Shanker, 1993). Is Mr. Shanker's view of a profession consistent with other's views of a profession? Other educators have defined the "tools of professional practice," as consisting of standards of excellence and voluntary accountability to those standards (Barringer, 1993, p. 21). Do the true "professions" maintain difficult entrance requirements, and, at least relatively positive rewards?

Professionalism for teachers may be impossible. Teaching is a mass occupation, teaching unions have a leveling effect, there are fiscal and political limits on raising teacher pay, and there is further political resistance from parents, and other taxpayers as to the "professional" control of "their" schools. Gary Sykes (1986) points out that given the potential roadblocks to teacher professionalization, their model should not be the success story of physicians, but rather the story of failure and frustration told by nurses. The goal should not be a position among the high professions, which is quite unlikely, but rather merely a more manageable improvement in the status of teachers.

Herbst (1989, p. 196) likewise concludes that teachers "can and should develop their own professionalism, not an imitation of the professionalism of doctors, lawyers, and school administrators, but through their own indigenous professional conduct in the classroom."

"Teaching is one of the learned professions, yet the work feels more blue collar than white" (Murphy, 1993, p. 645). Professionals are supposed to be distinguished from other workers by their command of a special body of knowledge and skills, by the unique contributions they make, by their greater freedom to organize their time, and by the autonomy to direct their own work. Teachers usually share none of these characteristics (Murphy, 1993). Further, the concept of a "professional" is rather undemocratic, and sometimes difficult to reconcile with the largely democratic ideals of the public schools. As far back as the beginning of the twentieth century, the National Education Association under the leadership of Nicholas Murray Butler, attempted to marry the traditional commitment to "service" of the public school teacher, with a more "modern" notion of professionalism, embracing educational training and scientific inquiry (Murphy, p. 51). Likewise, the AFT and its President in 1926, Mary Barker, strongly advocated professionalism. "Unless we ourselves consider our services valuable and show what we can do no one else will so recognize us" (Murphy, p. 118). If you are what you think you are, then teachers are most certainly "professionals." The primary purpose of the National Teachers Association (later to become the NEA), was, according to its preamble "to elevate the character and advance the interests of the profession" (Soder, 1990, p. 38).

The literature of professions and professionalization has tended to focus upon the noble ways in which the professions have contributed to society through their service, and by acting as stabilizing agents. Another common feature of the literature has been the desire among many authors to provide a "laundry list" of traits common to professions. Through an analysis of each list, given occupations were then either granted or denied entry. The specific literature concerning teacher professionalization encompasses arguments and opinions intended to resolve the issue of whether teaching is a trade, or a true "profession."

Chapter 7

Teacher Unionism/Professionalism Today

The literature on the determinants of unionization has, for the most part, found that a crucial factor in membership in a given state, is the status of that state's collective bargaining legislation. Those states with the most permissive legal environment also tend to report the highest levels of union membership (Kearney, 1984).

Teacher unionism arose, as most unionism does, because of real or perceived low wages, exclusion from the decision-making process, and other unsatisfactory working conditions. If teachers had felt that their working conditions were satisfactory, then the need for unionism in its common form would not have existed, and teachers would have been placated by professional associations alone. The transformation of teachers from passive "professionals" to union activists can be understood partially by the knowledge of teachers' perceptions of their standing in society. In studies that have considered the attitudes of teachers, the picture that emerges shows teachers wanting both respect from the public for the dedication they show to their profession, and the financial rewards they feel should come to skilled professionals (Eberts & Stone, 1984).

Teacher organizations may be a force in shaping the school as a professional organization, with a greater dependence on professional standards and a collegial rather than a heirarchical structure (Murphy & Hoover, 1976, p. 482). However, as the dates within the research indicate, the role of teacher organizations today is not substantially different than their role in 1976 and before.   Although, such organizations "may" still be a force in shaping the school as a professional organization, to date, such "shaping" has not been realized.

Today's emerging stance of the teacher organizations is not only a commitment to serve their members, but also to strengthen the institutions in which they work (at least that's their public stance). Whether this stance has emerged out of altruistic attitudes, or out of self-interest in improving schools and warding off such threats as privatization, is debatable and ultimately unimportant, so long as, in the end, the students benefit. It is inappropriate to criticize teachers or any other profession or vocation for the desire to maintain the viability of the organizations in which they gain their livelihood.   It cannot be reasonably expected that all members of each vocation should only be concerned with others to the detriment of themselves. "Maintenance of the organization has to be a prime objective of a leader, no matter what his or her personal beliefs; without the organization, no programs or goals can be met" (Urban, 1982, p. 109).

Many researchers have concluded that teacher unions have become the most powerful political constituency in education (Berube, 1988).   According to some, unions have had the effect of "freeing teachers from traditional authoritarian school administration" (Genck, p. xi).   This newfound "freedom" has allowed teachers to seek more participation in management, in order to improve performance and justify pay increases (Genck, p. xi). Most observers agree that teachers have benefitted from unions' influence in ending traditional authoritarian rule, but there is less agreement as to whether unions have contributed to achieving a more satisfactory management system to replace tradition (Genck, p. 63).

Because of their natural interest in education, and their resources, (monetary and numerically) teachers unions have become the chief representatives of education in American politics (Genck, p. 1). "As the union was the key to attaining even the minimal professional status our members now enjoy, so too is the union now the key to achieving the professionalization of teaching and the improvement of student learning" (Shanker, 1988).

Whatever else one thinks or knows about teaching, it is now one of the most heavily unionized occupations in society, certainly the most unionized white-collar occupation (Finn, 1985, p. 99). Nearly 90 percent of all the public school teachers in the U.S. belong to either the

NEA, the AFT, or to a handful of independent unions found in some communities (Finn, p. 99; Kearney, 1984; Keith & Girling, 1991). Unlike most unions which have experienced declining memberships in recent years, the NEA has enjoyed a 22% membership growth between 1981 and 1991; the AFT has enjoyed 37% growth during that same period (Weiler & Mundlak, 1993; Nulty, 1993). In ideal terms, unions as legal representatives can be "the means by which an occupational community can monopolize and protect areas of expertise" (Van Maanan & Barley, 1984). In practice, however, the actual range of issues over which unions have legal purview is limited: Unions command less occupational authority than do the organizations that represent the so-called professionalized occupations, such as medicine and law (Bascia, 1994; Haberman, 1986; Olson, 1965).

"Beyond Wages, Hours, and Working Conditions"

Another substantial difference between teachers' associations and most traditional unions lies in the desire of "professionals" to bargain over more items than the traditional subjects of wages, hours, and working conditions. They want to bargain about more effective school programs or other matters affecting educational policy (Anderson, 1968). Teachers' unions have already managed to expand the scope of bargaining wider than any other union (Kearney, 1984). Examples of the widening scope include: relief from non-teaching chores such as milk distribution; playground, cafeteria, bus, and hall supervision; and extra compensation for after-school administrative meetings, and parent-teacher conferences (Perry & Wildman, 1970).

Involving bargaining in the "mission of the agency," is a concept that seeks to use collective bargaining rather than the legislative process for effectuating change in social and economic policy (Anderson, 1968, pp.82-3). Put another way, if teachers' unions are permitted to bargain on matters of educational policy, it is conceivable that through successive contracts the autonomy of school boards could be eroded, and a large measure of control over educational policy shifted away from school boards toward teachers' unions (Kenai School District v. Education Association, 572 P.2d 416 (Alaska, 1977). In Kenai, the Alaska Supreme Court heard the arguments of the school board against allowing collective bargaining to intrude into educational policy areas. The argument against such involvement is based on an unconstitutional delegation of governmental power to the unions. In the case of <u>National Ed. Association of Shawnee Mission, Inc. v. Board of Ed.</u>, 512 P.2d 426, 435 (Kansas 1973), the Kansas Supreme Court drew the distinction between whether the issue bargained impacted the well-being of the individual teacher, as opposed to its effect on the operation of the school system as a whole. Although such a distinction is at least partially artificial, a matter is seen to be more susceptible to bargaining the more it deals with the economic interests of employees and the less it concerns professional goals and methods.

The desire of "professionals" to involve themselves in the decision-making process and "share" power with more traditional supervisory personnel is not a recent one. However, the fact that it still is pursued, using many of the same arguments of the 1970's, indicates that whatever gains teachers' associations have made have not come easily nor have they been the "sweeping" changes that many teachers feel are necessary. The encroachment of unionized professional workers into major decision-making impacting the production and delivery of services has been a continuing source of conflict between management and workers (Davey,et al., 1982). Further, it is a source of conflict that has fueled much of the literature concerning "empowerment," and ultimately the "professionalism" of teaching. Generally, the more professional the public employee, the more managerial decision-making is demanded (Metzler, 1973). The desire, on the part of teachers, to wrestle "control" over their profession away from administrators, boards, and other "non-teachers" is central to a study of "professionalism" generally, and teacher dismissals as evidence of that "professionalism" specifically.

The organizations with which teachers' have aligned themselves, provide the most assistance in analyzing what teachers' collectively want and how they attempt to satisfy those desires. The appeal of membership is strong as is indicated by the large numbers of teachers who belong. Whether teachers' organizations are practical organizations or more impractical "mass movements," is subject to debate. Some would argue that there is no difference, others feel that there is a significant difference between the appeal of a mass movement and the appeal of a practical organization (Hoffer, 1951).

Teachers' organizations have been appealing to some for the organizations' ability to provide practical self-interested assistance within the profession. To others, the appeal has been that of a mass movement toward the end of increasing the status of teachers broadly. A mass movement attracts and holds a following not because it can satisfy the desire for self-advancement, but because it can satisfy the passion for self-renunciation (Hoffer, 1951). Some members of both the AFT and the NEA are members mainly to identify themselves with the efforts and achievements of the worthy cause of teacher professionalization. Whether teachers in particular and educators generally joined one of the organizations primarily out of self-interest, or primarily out of a more "virtuous" professional desire, the organizations have each attempted to advance the "profession." The fact that their methods have often varied, and their membership is often contemptuous of the other, does not overwhelm the common desire that they share. While division does not lessen desire, it does diminish the standing of the "profession." In contrast to the medical and legal professions who are often mildly criticized for their self-protectionism, teachers are divided even among themselves. Such division is itself evidence of the lack of professionalism present in teaching (Dobay, 1988).

To understand the reasons that teachers, or any group, would participate in collective action of any kind, is to understand something about the theoretical argument that ties social class, political efficacy, and the educational factors of individuals together (Paulsen, 1991). To enter into and participate in a group, a given individual must feel a sense of belonging, and a reciprocal arrangement whereby the individual both gives and gets value from membership. Ronald Corwin, in a 1966 work, viewed teacher militancy as a stage in professionalization. He set forth three key factors necessary for a professional model in education: (1) the amount of autonomy to be gained for the vocation; (2) the ability to legitimize that autonomy with legal sanctions; and (3) the exclusive license to practice (Murphy & Hoover, 1976, p. 482). As of this date, these three factors have not been successfully implemented.

Although it is impossible to enter each member's mind to determine the exact thought processes that led to a given member's decision to join, the literature is replete with "reasons" for teacher unionism. Likewise, the literature in education and other fields contains "reasons" for organizing and taking collective action. The universal reason why people organize is "to enhance the individual through a collective presence" (Keith & Girling, 1991, p. 289). Like within the private sector, public sector workers join unions for economic, social, and psychological reasons (Coffinberger, 1981). They want higher wages and better benefits (economic), react favorably to pressure from their peers to join (social), and desire job security, participation in decision-making, and protection of their rights as workers (psychological) (Kearney, 1984, p. 15).

For teachers specifically, it is reasonably clear that the motivation was, and is, compounded of three elements: the desire to associate with one's peers for companionship, shared knowledge, and vocational betterment; the desire to improve one's own material well-being, job security, and working conditions; and the desire to strengthen the enterprise of public education itself, both for reasons of self-interest and for the benefit of the children one teaches and the society one inhabits (Finn, 1985, p. 101; see also inter alia, Urban, 1982). Based on a 1975 survey of state government workers in five states, Smith and Hopkins (1979) found that positive attitudes toward unions were related to dissatisfaction and lack of involvement with the job, lower occupational status, large organizations, and "negative life experiences" (e.g., raised in a poor family, little formal education) (Kearney, 1984, p. 16).

While changes are sought by teachers, they, not surprisingly, believe that these changes need to be reconciled with the present power structure within schools. Teachers, like governments, and businesses, do not favor revolution, but instead favor the perpetuation of their own cultures. "The hidden agenda in many schools is therefore to resist change" (Rothman, 1977, p. 64). It has been said that teachers unions are now placed in a situation in which they must defend the system as adequate, needing only extra money to improve. Since they wield much of the power within the public schools, they find it increasingly difficult to seriously consider proposals that might alter the status quo (Fantini, 1974). Any sweeping reforms suggested to improve the "profession," will likely be met with protectionist concerns. Raising teachers' salaries -- across the board and on the basis of merit -- is an obvious (probably even a necessary) means of supporting the professionalism of teachers, but alone that is not sufficient. Unions must also demand that schools be structured so as to sustain teachers in cultivating the capacity for critical thought within their classrooms (Gutmann, 1987).

There are aspects of a "mass movement" and aspects of a "practical organization" present in both the major education organizations, and as rational arguments have tended to achieve only tiny steps toward improvements in the lot of teachers, reason may have to share the pedestal with "true belief" as Hoffer might have put it. The readiness for united action and self-sacrifice is a mass movement phenomenon (Hoffer, p. 173).

Beyer et. al, (1989) add to the socialization studies of group membership by pointing out that society is continually re-created, although not always in the same form, through a shared understanding in which all of its members, to one degree or another, and within different frameworks, participate. "The function of educational scholarship is to understand these relationships as social constructions with historical antecedents" (p. 29). Teachers did indeed organize for reasons, many of which are put forth above. Beyond these "determinable" reasons however, lie many less clear reasons that all played a part in getting us to our present status.

Many, if not most Americans support unions in principle, but far fewer do so in practice. After all, what's not to support? Unions affirm the democratic vision in authoritarian companies by balancing the power of management and strengthening the relatively powerless employee. They guarantee due process in the workplace, free speech, more equitable distribution of rewards, and they stand for the rights and dignity of individuals (Maccoby, 1991). Despite such a glowing description, unions have been losing their clout, and public opinion about unions has been growing more and more unfavorable. Part of the reason for the downturn in public opinion, may have been because of the upturn in teacher strikes that has predictably followed the advance of teacher unionism. Between 1960 and 1965, public school teachers struck twenty-five times; betweeen 1975 and 1980, there were over a thousand strikes involving over a million teachers, according to the Bureau of Labor Statistics (Toch, 1991). Even though public employee strikes were illegal in most states, strike activity by public employees in general, and teachers in particular increased dramatically during the 1960's and 1970's (Partridge, 1992).

Are Teachers Members of Professional Associations or Unions?

The literature indicates that there is a significant difference in perception between what constitutes a "professional association" and a "union." Whether this difference exists in reality, is in doubt. "The issue is not unions vs. professional organizations, since it is difficult at best to validate the differences between them" (Vanderwerf, et al., 1979, p. 80). The blurring of lines between professional associations and unions is also illustrated by organizing efforts in "the real world."

Many graduate students at universities are, as of this writing, campaigning to organize student teaching and research assistants. In a letter to University of Iowa graduate students, dated November 29, 1993, among the benefits the organizers claimed were that "we gain respect in the eyes of the employer and enhance our own sense of dignity by voting for and then participating in the union, an organization of professionals..." The concept of a union as an "organization of professionals," has been troubling to many teachers and has impacted the history of the NEA.

Whatever the reality, even among educators themselves there is division about the need for "professional associations" as opposed to "unions." Many within the profession have advocated more organization among the rank and file teachers, but many who support organization oppose unionization.

> As a profession, education has the right to organize, but let it organize as a professional group as other professions have. Let not its organization be one that would take away any of its lofty ambitions and ideals but rather let it help to foster its true professional aims. Let its professional standards and qualifications be raised so that society will give further consideration and respect to it because society knows that it is their children who will benefit (Haley, 1946, reprinted 1993, p. 208).

The commissioner of education in 1962, Sterling McMurrin, viewed teacher organizations with trepidation at best, "national control of education by powerful professional organizations is as great a threat as is control by the federal government" (Beezley, 1963, p. 167).

The widely accepted belief, whether justified or not, that there is a distinguishable difference between a "professional association" and a "union," tends to exaggerate the portrayal of "professional associations" more positively than "unions." One criticism of teachers and their involvement with organizations has been due to the perceived inability of their organizations to choose between a role of "the union pursuing narrow self-interests, or a professional association that embraces greater public interests" (Flansburg, James, <u>Des Moines Register,</u> April 8, 1993). Although the necessity of making such a distinction as well as the validity of the distinction is arguable, there seems to be a commonly held perception that a union cannot simultaneously pursue self-interests and greater public interests. Therefore, garnering public support for any organizational goals would likely be more easily done by a professional association than a union.

The initial purpose of a professional association is usually to protect and enhance the profession through (1) defining its boundaries and setting entrance criteria, (2) lobbying with local government for varying degrees of autonomy or self-government by setting up and legalizing licensing procedures, and (3) conducting essentially public relations activities on behalf of the profession (Gilb, 1966). Other authors have described the purpose of professional organizations similarly, if less flatteringly. "Surely the purpose of a professional organization is to make a particular body of knowledge the exclusive possession of a particular body of men (more recently of women, too)" (Walzer, 1983, p. 156). Fenstermacher (1990) referred to this desire for exclusive control over a subject matter as the "mystification of knowledge." The effort of such organizations to remain exclusive is in part material; they aim to limit their numbers so that they can command high fees, and in part ego; they seek status (Walzer, 1983). "Professional knowledge is to organize social and private life, with the definitions 'owned' by particular communities of experts" (Popkewitz, 1987, p. 6). All of professionalism is necessarily then, a way of "drawing lines" (Walzer, p. 156).

Within the literature, there is a definite tendency among those within a given organization to consider their organization a "professional association." Conversely, there seems to be a tendency for those outside of a given organization to view that organization as a "union." Similarly, the literature leads inescapably to the conclusion, that like in society at large, the "best" education "reform" devised by individuals tends to place those individuals in the center of the movement. For example, there seems to be a definite trend among teachers and former teachers to place teachers at the center of their "reform" movements (See, inter alia, Rothman, 1977, p. 24). The same is true of businesspersons who tend to place business interests at the center of their "reform" proposals, or of politicians who tend to center their "reform" proposals on the "people," otherwise known as their constituents. Although self-interest does not, by itself, render any proposal invalid or even less valid than others, it is worthy of note.

In their considerations of professionalism, teacher union leaders, among them AFT President Albert Shanker, have referred to medicine and law as models for the teacher unions to follow (Shanker, The Making of a Profession Washington, D.C.:American Federation of Teachers, AFL-CIO, April, 1985). An examination of the AMA indicates that the AMA succeeded in uniting the medical profession into one organization, and in taking the initiative in reforming medical education (Berube, 1988). The NEA, as early as 1915, looked to the organizational model of the AMA, and sought to organize nationally by first having members align themselves with a state association, which would then affiliate itself with the national organization (Urban, 1982). Shanker, in a speech to the National Press Club in January, 1985, outlined a plan for a rigorous national entrance examination, modeled on law's bar examination (Toch, 1991, p. 143-44).

The complexity of teaching associations is symbolized by Shanker. He appears to be a devout "unionist" who nevertheless advocates many proposals that are decidely, and historically, anti-union. The fact that teachers are a group unlike any other seems to explain his support of career ladders, performance pay, and public school "choice," and reconciles his pro-union feelings with his understanding that a teachers' union cannot be like other unions if it is to flourish. Unlike other unions, the "product" is children, not cars or clothing (Rothman, 1977, p. 249).

Further evidence of the complexity of the teaching associations is illustrated by Chester Finn's membership within the AFT in the 1980's. Finn, a Reagan Department of Education appointee, seems an unlikely bedfellow of Albert Shanker, nevertheless he has said as recently as 1991, that "there aren't a dozen issues, foreign or domestic, on which I have any large quarrel with Albert Shanker" (Finn, 1991, p. 90).

The ideology of professionalism in education grew into a powerful anti-union slogan that effectively paralyzed and then slowed the unionization of teachers (Murphy, 1990). The teacher union movement has had an impact, if only incrementally, upon improving working conditions, wages, and in lobbying for educational legislation. At the same time, however, the movement has not become the engine for educational reform, that many founders undoubtedly had hoped it would be.

One answer for the "failure" of the teacher union movement to more positively influence educational reform, probably lies in the inability of teachers to form themselves into one union. According to David Seldon, a past president of the AFT, this lack of unity has focused the AFT and the NEA on their bitter rivalry and away from total concentration upon educational reform (Berube, 1988). Nelson &

Besag (1970) blamed the battle between the NEA and the AFT for heightening a lack of understanding of the interrelationship between school administrators and teachers, and thereby stifling cooperation. A merger of the two organizations is, and has been, often discussed (Elkin, 1979) but as of yet it has not been attained. In July of 1993, at the NEA's annual Representative Assembly, the delegates representing the approximately 2.1 million NEA members, voted to give NEA President Keith Geiger the green light to explore merger with the approximately 800,000 member AFT (NEA Higher Education Advocate, August, 1993).

The thought of collective activities in order to advance self-interests, challenged the perception that many teachers held about themselves and their colleagues, namely that entrance to the teaching "profession" was an altruistic choice. Sociologists have noted that the avowel of altruistic intent is often the basis for a field's bid for the legitimacy and prestige accorded to the traditional professions, medicine and law (Serow, 1993). While altruism remains a central theme in the ideology of professionalism (Kultgen, 1988), it is impossible to maintain that altruistic value orientations represent prevailing norms within the professions (Beyer, et al., 1989).

In the case of teaching, certain facts about the occupation tend to mitigate, (though not completely eliminate) skepticism about professional altruism (Serow, p. 198). The fact that teaching generally, and teachers specifically, have been perceived by large numbers of the public to be altruistic in career choice, has been both a benefit and a burden. While it is nice to be thought of as concerned with others first, it has created expectations for teachers that have been difficult to overcome. "Just as individuals derive identity and meaning from their personal values" (Katz, 1960), professions are identified and evaluated by those to which they subscribe (Koerin, 1977; Segal, 1992).

Etzioni (1988) subscribes to the theory that individual decisions typically reflect collective attributes and processes, having been made within the context created by one's membership in various groups. For teachers, membership in the profession of teaching and membership in the school as community provide the kind of collective attributes that hinder individual decision-making. "Connections are so important and the process of socialization as a result of memberships is so complete that the concept of individual decision maker appears to be more myth than reality" (Sergiovanni & Starratt, 1993).

AFT and NEA Differences (The Not So Great Divide)

To most observers, the AFT is a true union, while the NEA is somewhere within the spectrum of union-bargaining association-professional association. Bargaining associations are more likely to emphasize political action to influence decision-makers, while unions are more likely to concern themselves with working conditions (Burton & Thomason, 1988).

Until the 1960's, the NEA opposed the unionization of teachers, believing that unions and their emphasis on issues of working conditions and the use of strikes as legitimate weapons, reduced the extent to which teaching was considered a profession (Cole, 1969). The NEA actually furthered the notion that belonging to a union was unprofessional (Jarolimek, 1981). The perception was that "professional people are not workers, and unions are for workers" (Rothman, 1977, p. 249). It has long been an assumption that "while professional employees had a legitimate concern with the quality of their product, blue collar workers did not" (Blackburn & Busman, 1977, p. 81). With the prevalence of such belief, it is not difficult to understand the NEA's reluctance to allow teachers to be classified as "workers."

This reluctance on the part of the NEA was somewhat overcome in 1967, when the NEA issued a policy statement that affirmed the right of public employees to strike (Reid & Kurth, 1990). Collective bargaining itself presented the NEA with its deepest concern; it was an ideological construct that fundamentally challenged the association's long cherished concept of professionalism (Murphy, 1993). The AFT, in contrast, did not believe that concern for salary schedules and working conditions was incompatible with professionalism (Cole, 1969). The AFT had first advocated strikes as an option for teachers in 1963 (Reid & Kurth, 1990). Both organizations held the conviction that teaching needed to be "professionalized," they simply did not agree upon the best path toward that end.

Ironically, the NEA has moved slightly from its emphasis on "professionalism" toward unionism, whereas the AFT is now making stronger movement toward "professionalism" (Berube, 1988, p. 62). The two organizations and their evolution is symbolic of the schizophrenia within, and among, the teacher organizations. The organizations' successes and failures is likewise something of a paradox. Collective action has been beneficial in gaining higher wages and benefits, and providing a vehicle for broader political participation, yet it has also generated several unintended consequences, including, but not limited to having the effect of setting teachers apart as a special interest group engaged in pleading for higher salaries that necessarily require higher taxes (Ayers, 1992).

Albert Shanker, in his essay entitled "A Call For Professionalism" (Jan. 29, 1985, p. 7), told teachers that they must build a "second revolution in American public education" that will go beyond collective bargaining to an era of enlightened professionalism." His major goal in school reform is to redistribute more power to the teacher unions and ultimately, the teachers themselves (Berube, 1988).

In order to afford teaching the same professional status as many of the more "respected" vocations, there may well be a need to change some long-held perceptions. The word "unions" has carried the perception of representing the members of a trade or vocation, while "associations" have managed to carry with them a more "professional" status. Some authors, without stating specific distinctions between "unions" and "professional associations," have stated that "the union ideology, with its rigid categories of 'labor' and 'management,' is not easily applicable to a profession" (Berube, p. 178). However true that may be, the reasons are less clear why a "professional association" would lend itself more readily to appropriate representation of all members of a profession, however diverse those members might be.

It is likely that the "need" for many teachers to remain free of "unions," lies within the sociology of American society, for labor unions have often been viewed with little regard by great numbers of Americans. In the early 1800's and beyond, unions were regarded as criminal conspiracies per se because of their objective to raise wages and improve working conditions for the working classes. These objectives were seen by many, including the courts, as criminal (Dilts & Walsh, 1988; Commonwealth v. Pullis, 1806).

Much like the bar and medical associations, teachers' unions have supplied advanced education (through journals, workshops, institutes, and conventions); codes of ethics and behavior concerning how members of the profession should act and, especially, how they should expect others to act toward them; norms and qualifications for membership into the profession itself; and leadership, representation, and "voice" in the innumerable gatherings, events, and decisions of the larger society that bear on the profession and its work (Finn, 1985, p. 100). Although one primary goal of a professional association is in safeguarding the economic welfare of its individual practitioners (Cole, 1969), perceptions of a professional association tend to be somewhat different. For whatever reasons, the bar and medical associations are seldom considered "unions," while teachers' organizations are most often referred to as "unions" and less often as "professional associations."

It takes no great ability on the part of a researcher to find teacher's organizations referred to as both a union and a professional association. In the May 5, 1993, Education Week, a note concerning 1992-93 teacher salaries was interesting beyond its purpose, as it referred to an NEA report as a union report. (NEA "1992-93 Estimates of School Statistics," 1993, p. 3). Some local NEA affiliates think nothing of referring to themselves as a "teachers' union, while others contend that they are "associations" or "organizations" -- but not "unions" (Sharp, 1992, p. 234).

Whether one uses the word "union" or the words "professional association," it is evident that many of these organizations feel the need to contribute to political parties and individuals seeking election. Often these "special interests" tend to receive negative press, particularly when the interests are determined by the public to represent "unions." The need, perceived or real, to contribute to political causes does not seem to distinguish between unions, and professional associations. According to the Federal Election Commission, as reported in the May 24, 1993, Newsweek, the National Education Association ranked third among contributors, behind the Teamsters, and the American Medical Association, and just ahead of the National Rifle Association, the National Association of Realtors, and the Association of Trial Lawyers of America ("Top 10 PAC Spenders," 1993, p. 6).

The negative implications surrounding PACs run deep. "The NEA and AFT are among the largest and most politically sophisticated of the establishment organizations,... their PACs are among the richest, right up there with the postal workers, the trial lawyers, and the bankers" (Finn, 1991, p. 193). Whether Finn's neglect in mentioning the AMA was intentional is uncertain, his selective list is useful however, in its use of the word "establishment" to describe teachers' organizations. The use of the word "establishment" to negatively describe teachers' organizations by a former member of a presidential administration (more commonly seen as "establishment,") is quite indicative of the extent of negativism associated with PACs generally, and education PACs specifically. This study will leave it to the reader to draw any conclusions from PAC spending, but if "professional associations" exist only to advance the interests of their profession, the cost to advance those interests is remarkably similar to the cost "unions" see as necessary in protecting their members and in striving for better wages, hours, and working conditions.

Teachers are still often thought to be "unworthy" of "professional" status (Warren, 1989, p. 7). Because of the lack of "status" that accompanies teaching, there may lie a valid need beyond camaradirie, for teachers to seek membership in associations for the purpose of improving their standing. At least arguably, improving the standing of the teaching profession is necessary to improve the quality of education. In order to improve the standing of the "profession," it must be determined if teaching is in fact a "profession."

Chapter 8

Changes in Teacher Education

"Efforts to professionalize teaching should both build teacher commitment and improve curriculum and instruction" (Firestone, 1993, p. 7). "If reforms in teacher education, changes in teacher licensing, and a move to advanced certification achieve their goals, perhaps education will at last become a true profession" (Lewis, 1993, p. 589).

Almost all reports on professional education reject the separate trade school concept, and indicate that only in a university setting can the requisite interdisciplinary and interdepartmental work be carried on. Professional faculties resemble professors rather than practitioners (Mayhew, 1971, p. 29). This means that for the most part professional curricula emphasize basic science and theory rather than applied work. Only grounding in basic theory can allow the practitioner to continue to grow and to fit new applications into his/her broad theoretical framework (Mayhew, 1971). If Mayhew is correct, and as of 1996, it appears he is, then there might be hope for those without "practical" experience within the field of education to enter the "profession," and strengthen it by our diversity and desire to "practice" the art. Other "professions" require training and entrance requirements, but not prior experience within the field. To so require experience implies that much of the profession is learned "on the job," which seems to run counter to "professional" thinking.

Any curricular demands and changes, however noble and

practical, must bear some reasonable relationship to the rewards and lifestyle of the profession. "The economics of the profession must change as rapidly as does teacher education or the entire development effort is doomed" (Herndon, 1983, p. 42). Students might benefit from a richer program of study, however, students would be unlikely to tolerate a larger, more expensive program in view of the rewards that the practice of the profession actually provides (Mayhew, 1971, p. 82). The dilemma for education is how to avoid such a "catch 22." To increase status and "professionalism" an expanded and more selective period of training may be required, however, without greater rewards upon completion, aspiring "professionals" would probably gravitate toward medicine, law and other more outwardly "rewarding" career choices. One indicator of the role and scope of a profession is what it transmits to practitioners in the formal education process (Roeder & Whitaker, 1993). Consensus upon what needs to be included within professional educational programs for teaching is important in order to make more uniform professional standards possible.

"Empowerment/Site Based Decision-Making"

"Empowerment," or "site-based decision-making" is one of the school reform/professionalism literature's favorite terms, and as such it is included in this review of professionalism. The second wave of educational reform (the first having been calls for higher standards for teachers and students), consisted largely of calls for more teacher "empowerment." Other writings referred to "empowerment" as decentralized decision-making or site or school-based management. This study will use the terms interchangeably, if only to illustrate the common practice within the reform literature. What empowerment means is "to share authority" (Nyberg, 1990, p. 62). The "empowerment" approach to raising the social status and pay of teachers consists of a change in focus to a concentration upon increased responsibility and decision-making power.

The literature seems to suggest that much of the innovation in the field of education, lies not in discovering new ideas, but merely in discovering new names for old ideas. In any case, in 1986 the Carnegie Task Force on Teaching as a Profession implored local school districts to find ways to give "teachers a greater voice in school decisions" (Clark, 1993, p. 183). The Carnegie proposals led the second wave of reform (Darling-Hammond, 1988, p. 58). "In policy terms, the second wave reformers suggest greater regulation of teachers -- ensuring their competence through more rigorous preparation, certification, and selection -- in exchange for the deregulation of teaching -- fewer rules prescribing what is to be taught, when, and how" (Darling-Hammond, p. 59).

The site-based management movement grew out of research suggesting that school autonomy is associated with school effectiveness (Purkey & Smith, 1985). Support for the idea has also come from studies that found education reform was most effective when implemented by people who felt a sense of ownership and responsibility for the reform (Fullan, 1991). "For school-site management to succeed, it must be developed with the specific goal of creating a professional work environment for teachers. Without this goal, school-site management may become just another bureaucratic mode of control in the guise of reform" (Conley & Bacharach, 1991, p. 127).

If teaching is ever to be effectively "professionalized," site-based management appears to be the key factor. A professional in order to "practice" his or her craft would undeniably need some degree of autonomy. Legally, however, the doctrine of "respondeat superior" would likely hamper a tremendous shifting of responsibility toward the teacher. Some decision-making responsibility may shift from the central office to the school site, the liability for legal action, however, does not (Dunklee & Shoop, 1993). It is difficult, if not impossible to "professionalize" teaching if within greater autonomy is the underlying principle that the professional teacher should have "input" but not decision making power over educational goals, input and interpretive involvement in evaluation, but "primary authority" over only teaching methodology (Holmes & Wynne, 1989).

Among the earliest "demands" of teachers' unions was the desire for a greater role in the administration of schools and the determination of educational policies, by granting teachers more control over their work (Gutmann, 1987). "Teachers have not been professional. We haven't been treated that way and indeed in the real sense of the word, this has not been a profession because a profession is basically made up of people who are experts and by virtue of the expertise that they have, they have a very high degree of decision-making power" (Shanker, 1993, p. 680). Providing the "workers" with more say in how the company runs is a common theme of unionism. Accordingly, the AFT has from its inception sought "democracy in education, education for democracy" (Cheng, 1981, p. 27). Desiring more say is common among both union and nonunion teachers, as both generally prefer a greater degree of teacher participation in administrative decisions (Eberts & Stone, 1984). A possible undesired "side-effect" of more participation is that as teachers grow more visible in their desire for more "power" over decision-making, they will probably no longer be exonerated from the responsibility for "bad" decisions made by boards and administrators (Lortie, 1975, p. 222).

Approaches to school-based management have not been uniform (in keeping with the literature on school reform). The debate over teacher empowerment in the literature has, for the most part, polarized into a debate over autonomy versus accountability (Nyberg, 1990).

The difficulties in implementing decentralized decision-making in states with collective bargaining provisions, lies in the willingness of the exclusive bargaining representatives to agree on the vague concept of shared power between building level administrators and a majority of a building's teachers. The literature speaks of the well-intentioned efforts to involve teachers in decision-making, having actually exacerbated tensions between union and management, teacher and principal (Barth, 1988, p. 130). The ethics of such a plan also need to be considered, since it seems to imply that the governance of school buildings within districts might differ radically. California has tried, in select districts, an "educational policy trust agreement" in which traditional labor relations give way to a system in which joint action on school reform issues is contemplated between labor and management (Kerchner & Koppich, 1991). Whether such a radical departure from tradition can be expanded is in doubt, as is whether such a method is actually such a radical departure.

Proponents of "empowerment" tend to say that school based management has the potential to improve employee morale, encourage employee loyalty, improve the delivery of educational services, decrease turnover, reduce absenteeism, and reduce adversarial labor relations (See inter alia Walker & Roder, 1993). Other advocates speak of the symbolic value in the messages sent to teachers, parents, and the community, that teachers, as professionals, are worthy of regard and respect (Lieberman, Saxl, and Miles, pp. 165-66; Barth, 1990, pp. 130, 132, 138). Weiss (1993) pointed out that symbolism can operate negatively as well, as what she refers to as "shared decision making" may give teachers merely a "semblance of authority while real authority remains securely anchored in the principal's office or the district headquarters" (p. 70).

"Potential" benefits aside, there does not exist hard evidence that school-based management has a positive impact on student achievement or that it attains its objectives (Malen, 1990). The converse is also true as there is also no hard evidence that it is a negative for students (Weiss, 1993). Beyond the lack of hard evidence available concerning the benefits or costs of "empowerment," lies the criticism in many thoughtful studies that the teacher power in the present wave of reform is "derived power." Far from actual power, it is the granting of a license by others to act somewhat free of direction in specified areas of performance (Cooper, 1988, p. 50). Within the literature, is the remarkable ability on the part of proponents of "empowerment" to promote "professionalization" as a necessary corrolate to more power, yet refer to teachers as "employees" in extolling the virtues of "empowerment" as a morale builder.

The term "empowerment" can itself be a term synonymous with professionalization (Maeroff, 1988). To some, all professionals desire "participative and supportive management, autonomy and independence in decision making, and for measures of performance that separate outstanding contributors from average ones and that are used as a basis for compensation" (Genck, 1991, p. 61). Although sweeping generalizations that use the term "all" are usually far too inclusive, there does seem to be a body of evidence that indicates that Genck's belief is valid. That certainly most, if not all teachers, wished that these elements played a greater role in their field, and if these elements were present, the profession would be elevated in all ways, including pay. Evidence of Genck's assertion lies in a 1988 NEA study which indicated that 63 percent of the teachers studied wanted more influence in hiring, testing, budget, spending, and faculty assignment decisions (Goens & Clover, 1991).

Teachers more often speak of professionalism in terms of environmental conditions than of standards and dispositions (Barringer, 1993). "Professionals usually have a sense of authority about what they do and are recognized as experts in their fields. They feel good about themselves and are respected by others. The empowerment of teachers has to do with their individual deportment, not their ability to boss others. It is the power to exercise one's craft with confidence and to help shape the way that the job is done" (Maeroff, 1988, p. 4).

Reform through such restructuring, and the granting of power to those below is seen as a threat to some, and a panacea to others (First, 1992). David (1990) suggests that "pressure is on school districts to restructure...to decentralize authority, create more professional workplaces, and focus resources on teaching and learning" (p. 211).

The taxpayers continuing revolt against the public schools ensures that school boards will continue to have difficulty finding the money to pay for substantial salary improvements for teachers. The lack of funding is directly related to the public's ongoing disappointment with the "results" coming from the public schools. Such frustration with public education has added to the pressure that the NEA and AFT are under to increase teacher "professionalism." Because of this pressure, the AFT at least, has responded by supporting site-based decision-making, a policy that they had previously opposed (Keith & Girling, 1991). In 1985, Albert Shanker, President of the AFT, stated that "collective bargaining has been a good mechanism, and we should continue to use it. But we must now ask whether collective bargaining will get us where we want to go" (Peck, 1988, p. 33).

The Role of Tenure in Teacher Professionalism

The goal of tenure as originally introduced by the NEA in 1885, was to extend the principles of civil service to the teaching profession (Kuenzbi, 1945). Essentially the theory is that tenure should protect teachers, promote good order and further the best interests of the school and the state, by preventing the removal of teachers for political motives. Tenure laws were first established because of the high-handed way school authorities dealt with teachers (Jarolimek, 1981; Gross, 1988). Tenure laws can help maintain a good educational system by ensuring the stability and security of satisfactory teachers and by outlining orderly procedures for the dismissal of unsatisfactory teachers (Fischer, Schimmel, Kelly, 1991). "The tenure principle represents a type of social contract in which society protects the position of the teacher and the teacher has fewer renumerations and perquisites than higher risk positions" (Jarolimek, 1981, p. 284).

In most situations, a teacher acquires tenure as established by state law. Most states have laws that outline the requirements for tenure, and these laws generally require teachers to undergo a period of probationary service before they can become tenured or "permanent" teachers (Fischer, et al., 1991, p. 18). The key difference between tenured and untenured teachers in most states is the fact that to dismiss a tenured teacher, school officials must have a "just cause."   Teacher tenure laws generally list specific infractions that constitute "just cause" for dismissal. In contrast, the dismissal of an untenured teacher at the end of a contract period, needs to include no reason whatsoever.

Regardless of the procedures required under a given state's law, the U.S. Supreme Court has ruled that teachers are entitled to notice and hearing if their termination deprives them of "property" or "liberty" interests under the due process clause of the Fourteenth Amendment. The Court defined these terms in the case of <u>Board of Regents v. Roth</u>, 408 U.S. 564 (1972).

The assumption made in some of the literature that tenure laws are outdated and force public schools to put up with incompetent teachers (see Jarolimek, 1981), does not seem to mesh with the reality of the state codes and with the results of most dismissal litigation. The reality is that, although tenure laws necessarily may delay the dismissal of a teacher, they do not require schools to continue the employment of ineffective or incompetent teachers (Citron, 1985).   Before tenured teachers may be dismissed, school boards must simply show cause why they are not fit to teach (Fischer, et al., 1991). Like so many areas within the education literature, the concept and practice of tenure has been both praised and condemned at various periods and from various sources.

The Role of Teacher Licensing in Teacher Professionalism

Education has not equalled medicine or architecture in terms of accreditation of practitioners because education never developed a common set of expectations for teachers (Arthur Wise, as quoted in Lewis, 1993, p. 588). In addition, the difficulties and challenges of teaching were minimized, and, with the value of the work set low, "the price of the labor was kept low" (Lewis, p. 588). To a great extent, the strength and reputation of a profession depends upon its professional accrediting body. National accreditation might provide for consensus about standards which every other established profession now has (Roth, 1992). "If we do not invent our own future for the profession of teaching and teacher education, others will invent it for us" (Wise & Leibbrand, 1993, p. 133).

Freidson (1986) referred to licensing as "credentialing," the most impressive forms of which produce an "occupational cartel," which gains and preserves monopolistic control over a supply of a good or service in order to enhance the income of its members by protecting them from competition by others. An analogy Freidson used was that of the "gatekeeper" to the profession, only allowing certain persons in to perform the tasks of that profession. Collins (1979) referred to an "occupational community with strong controls and defenses." Teachers, despite their occupational control in terms of having licenses provided by the state, cannot survive economically by offering their services as entrepreneurs to individuals in the external labor market, they instead need jobs in the internal labor markets of organizations that attract individual clients in large batches (Freidson, p. 71). Such a significant difference between teachers and many other "professionals" who are able to support themselves on an individual basis cannot be diminished as a major reason "professionalism" for teachers cannot be of the same "type" as "professionalism" for doctors and lawyers.

Most states require that a teacher hold a valid state certificate, and be subject to additional requirements imposed by the school board (Strahan & Turner, 1987). Certification was intended to develop professional standards and, like tenure, improve the teaching profession. Generally, the certification process is the legal device by which the state assures the public that candidates who present themselves for teaching positions possess the minimum personal and professional qualifications (Strahan & Turner, p. 46). Licensed professionals, specifically teachers, are obliged to avoid the forms of incompetence about which there is societal consensus (Bull, 1990). Beyond any consensus, however, competence is in the eye of the beholder. School boards in this country are the "beholders."

Licensure, gives a teacher the legal authority and power to teach, but the process that the teacher has undertaken to become licensed may initiate the teacher into the world of bureaucracy and actually undermine the power to teach (Ayers, 1992). Like most things in the field of education, the need for greater professionalization through higher and more rigid standards, is highly debatable. The literature is split between those who feel professionalization demands licensing agencies to consist of "professionals" within the field, and those who feel democratic education and effective accountability to the public supercedes any value of keeping licensing decisions within the "family" (Bull, 1990, p. 120). Chester Finn, who served as assistant secretary for educational research and improvement in the closing years of the

Reagan administration, has stated:

> the profession is fighting back and trying to regain control, and it is doing so under the heading of professionalization and decentralization and autonomy and school site management, and I think it's a very sophisticated campaign by the profession to put itself back in the driver's seat. It carries with it the suggestion that the lay policy makers should butt out. And I think that would be a horrendous blunder for this country (Finn, as cited by Fenstermacher, 1990, p. 130).

Since the Reagan administration was not widely known for its love of unions, perhaps Finn's views on "unions" might be perceived as somewhat politically tainted. Politics aside, however, he does seem to frame the debate concerning the democratization vs. professionalization discussion in teacher credentialing, as a war between teachers and policymakers.

While professions do have some privilege in their standing, the courts insistently claim to be the ultimate arbiter of entitlement to it (Freidson, 1986). "By and large, the deciding criterion for privilege seems to be recognition by the courts of some form of knowledge, skill, or experience sufficiently specialized that the ordinary person -- the 'reasonable man' in legal tradition -- cannot be expected to know, possess, or be able to practice it adequately" (Freidson, p. 93). The separation between a profession and those outside of the profession is the basis for licensing, and the basis for the profession itself.

Whatever the impact upon students of the licensure process, it seems difficult to argue with the necessity of holding teachers up to certain standards and of removing incompetent teachers. The argument in the literature is not about requiring and maintaining licensing standards, it is about who should be on such a licensing agency admitting teachers to practice.

Powers of School Boards

Boards are empowered with general and supervisory control over the government and management of the schools and school property within a given district (Wiles & Bondi, 1985). Boards have tremendous discretion in setting and implementing policy so long as that policy does not conflict with state and federal law (Wiles & Bondi, p. 61; Maddaus, 1992; Jacobsen, et al., 1972).

The power to dismiss a teacher generally rests with the school board as prescribed by statute. In the absence of statutory authority, it may be exercised as an implied power by that body possessing the authority to employ (Jacobsen, et al., 1972). The power of boards may be seen in the reluctance of courts to overturn their decisions. "When there are challenges courts do tend to uphold local school boards" (Reutter, 1985).

How much "improvement" in public education can be made through "improved" school boards is debatable. More skepticism toward schemes for innovation and bureaucratic growth, and more sensitivity to the morale of teachers might be a starting point (Dobay, 1988). The importance of the persons making up the board should not be understated, however. Former President Carter (1992, pp. 187-88) addresses a significant concern about the membership of public school boards when he states:

> Many public school boards have come to be dominated by affluent members whose children attend the community's private schools. Inevitably, their interests tend to be more focused upon holding down property tax rates that finance schools than on providing adequate support to enhance the curriculum in the schools that their children do not attend.

The group of persons making up the board is legally responsible for overseeing the schools and is therefore often called upon to make important decisions for their school organizations. Depending upon a given school's impact in a community, the school board is the most powerful agency through which community needs and wishes are represented (Banks, 1976; First, 1992). Generally, however, that group of persons is rather "remote and only sets broad policies, which may or may not be carried out depending on conditions" (Brookover & Erickson, 1975, p. 179). This remoteness is perceived by many teachers to be at the root of any employment difficulties they might face. "In their authorized role as employer, many school board members probably regard teachers as hired labor with limited professional status" (Brookover & Erickson, p. 182). Dobay (1988, p. 50) referred to boards as "guardians of the public trust... with a special responsibility to reverse disastrous policies undermining teacher effectiveness and academic standards."

State laws define the authority of school boards in terminating the employment of school personnel. Generally, these laws specifically enumerate the causes for which a teacher may be terminated (McCarthy,

1987). Any teacher, tenured or not, may be discharged during his or her contract if there is sufficient cause to justify the termination (Strahan & Turner, 1987). "Sufficient causes" tend to vary from state to state. The courts tend to hold to the view that where a statute sets forth specific grounds, they are exclusive, and other grounds are precluded by implication. From a practical point of view, this protection is minimal because many states have included within their statutes extremely broad grounds (Morris, 1989).

The right of a school board to determine the fitness of teachers has been well established; in fact, courts have declared that school boards have a duty as well as a right to make such determinations (McCarthy, p. 379). The U.S. Supreme Court in Adler v. Board of Educ., 342 U.S. 485, 493 (1952), held that "school authorities have the right and duty to screen the officials, teachers, and employees as to their fitness to maintain the integrity of the schools as a part of ordered society." Maintaining this "integrity" has often meant that teachers were held to a higher standard of conduct than persons not in such "influential" positions. According to the Alaska Supreme Court in 1964, "a teacher's recognized duty is to conduct himself in such a way as to command the respect and good will of the community, though one result of his choice of vocation may be to deprive him of the same freedom of action enjoyed by persons in other vocations." Watts v. Seward School Bd., 395 P.2d 372, (Alaska 1964). Likewise, the Nevada Supreme Court, has stated that "a teacher's influence upon his pupils is not limited to what he says and does in the schoolroom, and a teacher's right to teach cannot depend solely upon his conduct in the schoolroom." Meinhold v. Clark County School Bd. of School Trustees of Clark County School Dist., 506 P.2d 420, 89 Nev. 56, cert denied 94 S.Ct. 247, 414 U.S. 943, 38 L.Ed.2d 167. (Nev. 1973).

For our purposes, it is essential to remain cognizant of the fact that school boards possess tremendous discretion, but not absolute discretion. The sources of control over school boards can be broken down generally into five areas: (1) Constitutional provisions; (2) Legislative enactments; (3) Rules and regulations set forth by the state board of education; (4) The courts and their interpretations of statutes and cases brought before them, as well as the given state's attorney general's interpretations of questions of law; and (5) Societal demands (Wiles and Bondi, 1985). The "thin line" between representative democracy as expressed by the decisions of school boards, and collective bargaining which appropriately precludes citizen participation is not always clear. The New Jersey Supreme Court, in the case of <u>Ridgefield Park Education Association v. Ridgefield Park Board of Education</u>, 78 N.J. 144, 393 A.2d 278, 287, (1978), went so far as to say that "the very foundation of representative democracy would be endangered if decisions of significant matters of governmental policy were left to the process of collective negotiation, where citizen participation is precluded."

Teacher professionalism, and site-based management proposals (which this review has addressed beginning with page 61 and 112 respectively) also raise issues of concern to school boards. Teacher professionalism proposals suggest that teachers should run and manage schools (Odden, 1992), a suggestion that fits with professionalism (Sykes, 1991) but runs counter to the traditional lay control of American schools (McDonnell, 1991).

Self-Regulation

The discussion of the professionalization of teaching, needs to be kept in the context of the real world. The tradition of school boards overseeing schools, and community ownership of the schools is powerful. School boards are not likely to readily accept handing over their power to teachers acting autonomously within the schools, even if teachers become "better" (Judge, 1988, p. 228). Having said that, much literature exists concerning the "self-regulation" of teachers, and that literature is worthy of addressing.

Any vocation that seeks to attain "professional" status must have provisions whereby its members have the ability to police themselves. A "profession" must necessarily limit itself to a group of "selected" members that must achieve a certain minimum status in order to enter, and be subject to expulsion should circumstances warrant. The history of the professions of law and medicine show that one way in which they achieved positions of prestige, was through placing increasingly tighter restrictions on entrance (Cole, 1969). It is part of the American ideology that the longer one has to go to school for a profession, the higher that profession's standing (Hughes, 1973). "A major task of teacher education is that of elevating the level of teaching practice from the personal to the professional through the expansion and utilization of research, professional wisdom, and logical analysis" (Denemark, as cited in Herndon, 1983, p. 39). The professions of medicine, and to a lesser degree, law, have increased their "prestige" by placing relatively tight restrictions on entrance to the profession.

The desire of persons to be considered "professional" is consistent with the increase in status that tends to accompany the "professions." Because of this strong desire to attain professional status, the number of "professionals" present today is markedly higher than in years past. Persons who seek to exploit their "expertise," such as insurance agents, financial planners, accountants, and so forth have now risen to "professional" levels within our society. Does this trend toward professionalization, or at least the desire for professionalization, diminish the traditional professions, or further enhance them by this flattery?

Educators must, almost always, "practice" their "profession" within the constraints of an organization. Within an organization, an educator must reconcile the need for providing for the best interests of the "client" while simultaneously acting in accordance with the interests of the institution. Sergiovanni writes of the emphasis on "doing things right, at the expense of doing the right things" (Sergiovanni, 1992, p. 4). Although Sergiovanni's focus was leadership, the value of the concept to the profession generally is found in the difficult reconciliation that teachers must accomplish in their roles as professionals, but professionals within the confines of a school.

Educators face stringent limitations upon their authority and their professional autonomy because of the great extent to which they are subject to the control of nonprofessionals. A profession generally claims a broad mandate to define what ails its clients and the public with respect to some problems and actions (Hughes, et al., 1973). Professions tend to protect their "territory" against outside interference by lay people (Hughes, et al., 1973, p. 10). Educators, who are ultimately controlled by a school board which sets policies for a given district, quite clearly do not have such power to prevent "outside" interference. The "outside" interference is, in fact, central to the fashion in which education has been distributed historically in America. In addition, employment in large-scale bureaucracies sharply modifies professional career progression. Instead of career advancement taking place through systems controlled by professional colleagues, career advancement becomes a matter of progressing through heirarchies in which control is shared with or dominated by nonprofessionals (Scott, 1965; Alutto & Belasco, 1976, p. 80).

The professionalization of teachers by increasing their autonomy and authority, among the literature that seeks "empowerment," may run counter to the concept of service to the public interest that "professions" claim. In other public service occupations, autonomy is the problem that professionalism is meant to address. It is precisely because practitioners operate autonomously that safeguards to protect the public interest are necessary (Darling-Hammond, 1988). Members of the public will not, and probably should not, trust an occupation to govern itself, unless they can be assured that all practitioners will possess the requisite knowledge, ability, and commitment to do what is best for their clients (Darling-Hammond, 1988, p. 65). The basic reason that much of the school reform, particularly the first "wave," concentrated on efficiency, uniformity, and prescriptive, top-down management procedures, is and was because policy makers simply do not trust teachers to make responsible, educationally appropriate choices and judgments (Darling-Hammond, 1988, p. 63). Critical again, seems to be the distinction between the one-on-one "choice" relationships of practitioner and client in the professions of medicine and law, and the one-on-group "forced" relationship of teacher and students in education. The distinction is significant enough to have prevented true "self-regulation" in education, and the arguments in the literature on professionalism, have not satisfactorily overcome the reasoning used by policymakers in making that critical distinction.

General organizational characteristics of institutions employing professionals may account for modifications in the degree of professionals' militancy (Kornhauser, 1963; Alutto & Belasco, 1976). Not all teachers share the same degree of "militancy," or desire to unite into more powerful bargaining units. As individuals vary, so too do organizations. Since there must exist, at some level, a dissatisfaction among workers to feel the need to unite, those workers who are more dissatisfied with the present will tend to more readily embrace united actions. Further, militancy in labor is related to militancy in other components of society. It is fostered by a pervasive attitude that institutions in general, and schools in particular, are not functioning properly (Cresswell, 1976, p. 7).

Professional Relationships & Unauthorized Practice

Professional relationships tend to require "distance" between the professional and the client.   In education, this requirement and its inherent ambiguity has added a painful irony in the history of teaching. Early in the twentieth century, teachers were damned for being too close to the community.   Later, they were damned for distancing themselves from it (Murphy, 1990).   There always is ambiguity present in the requirement of professionals to be detached yet caring. The problem of detachment in such an occupation runs counter to some perceptions of professionalism. "Teachers who are truly professional...are concerned, are friendly, are caring. They know that professionalism calls for... the teacher never getting used to a child's pain.   They know that professionalism does not call for becoming hard-hearted with experience but becoming more receptive to the human condition" (Rothman, 1977, p. 86). Similarly, Fenstermacher (1990, p. 146-7) has said "the need for teachers who are enlightened moral agents and moral educators calls for close, caring, connected association between teachers and students." Smith (1990) stated "there is no decent, adequate, respectable education...without personal involvement by a teacher with the needs...of his or her students" (p. 7).

Lawyers, as professionals, have the obligation and privilege of "policing themselves," in determining the appropriate degree of personal contact with a client. Many of the cases in which these professionals face discipline specifically involve the crossing of the invisible line between caring detachment and personal involvement. The literature commonly expresses the fear that professionalization will mean detachment which will mean less interest in children and consequently, less effective teaching.

The accepted "professions" of law and medicine have a monopoly upon the practice of their respective crafts, "gatekeeping" as Freidson (1970, 1986), refers to it. The unauthorized practice of law or medicine results in the prosecution of the party engaged in such unauthorized practice. Beyond the obvious requirement of licensure, even those properly licensed may face unpleasant circumstances professionally for engaging in activities that the individual is not competent to handle. The potential for liability for malpractice faces any lawyer or doctor who fails to perform to the level reasonable within that community. Further, however, cases of "internal" reprimand exist when lawyers engage in "representation which he or she knows or should reasonably know they are not competent to handle" <u>Committee on Professional Ethics & Conduct v. Morris</u>, 490 N.W.2d 806 (Iowa

1992). Professionalization of teaching will necessarily draw upon the standards, good and bad, set down by the historically accepted professions. Arguably, with increased potential for liability and other risks gained in reaching professional status, teachers might consider the ramifications of the "unauthorized practice of teaching."

Teacher Malpractice Considerations

In keeping with the desire to prevent "unauthorized" practitioners from infringing upon the role of "authorized" educators, must be the requirement of establishing certain minimum standards that these "authorized" educators must not fall below. Relatively clear guidelines must be established to allow professionals to "practice" their craft to the exclusion of non-professionals. Within the established guidelines, should be the knowledge that any increase in professionalism, real or perceived, may bring an increase in potential liability for the professional who fails to meet these standards.

Thus far, the tort of malpractice has not met with much acceptance in the field of education. The term "educational malpractice" refers to an attempt to hold the educator liable and accountable to provide a quality education to students (Loscalzo, 1985, p. 595). <u>Peter W. v. San Francisco Unified School District</u>, 60 Cal. App. 3d 814, 131 Cal. Rptr. 864 (1976), was the first and probably most widely publicized suit for "educational malpractice" (Loscalzo, 1985, p. 596). In that case, a high school graduate sued his school seeking recovery for deprivation of basic academic skills. He graduated, but had the reading, writing, and math skills of an eighth grader. The California Court of Appeals ruled that "recognized public policy considerations alone negate an actionable duty of care in persons and agencies who administer the academic phases of the educational process." Similarly, in <u>Donohue v. Copiague Union Free School District</u>, 391 N.E.2d 1352 (1979), the New York Court of Appeals set forth the oft cited precedent that "as a matter of public policy, courts simply should not become involved in the professional judgment of educators in determining appropriate methods of teaching." Essentially then, such a claim may be formally pleaded, but liability is precluded by public policy (Loscalzo, 1985). Every court addressing the issue has refused to hold private or public schools liable for failure to adequately educate, when the plaintiffs argued that the defendant breached a common law or statutory duty to the student. See Joel E. Smith, Tort

Liability of Public Schools and Institutions of Higher Learning for Educational Malpractice, 1 A.L.R.4th 1139, 1140 (1992). Nevertheless, with any increase in professionalism, may go a corresponding increase in acceptance of plaintiff's claims for educational malpractice.

Proof of causation in educational malpractice claims is nearly impossible, as substandard academic performances may and do have numerous causes. Teachers know only too well of the tendency for parents and the public at large to blame teachers for students' poor performances, but to ignore the role of teachers in the successes of good students. The impact upon a child's education of the environment surrounding that child outside of the school is often cited as the leading cause of poor performance by that child's teachers. His or her parents, however, may be more likely to blame that child's teachers. Abdicating responsibility serves no useful purpose, however, it is mentioned here to illustrate the difficulty teachers are faced with in providing for the best interests of individual students while simultaneously attempting to provide for the best interests of a classroom full of students. Teachers should be aware that despite the widespread reluctance of courts to intervene in questions of educational policy, and despite the absence of a uniformly accepted reasonable standard of care on the part of teachers, courts have repeatedly and in a variety of contexts appraised the strength or weakness of a particular program, environment, and mode of instruction [see generally the desegregation cases in which courts have determined that racially unbalanced schools may not provide adequate instruction (Jerry, 1981, p. 203)].

Evolution of Teachers' Employment Relationships

Historically, teachers have been allowed fewer personal freedoms than those allowed other citizens. Horace Mann, then Secretary of the Massachusetts Board of Education, in 1840, wrote that "the school committee are sentinels stationed at the door of every schoolhouse in the state, to see that no teacher ever crosses its threshold, who is not clothed, from the crown of his head to the sole of his foot, in garments of virtue..." (Mann "Fourth Annual Report," 1840, from Fraser, 1989, pp. 120-21). Teachers have been expected to promote learning, good citizenship, and morality, while being themselves models of educational attainment and cultural refinement (Warren, 1989, p. 7). Terry Herndon, executive director of the NEA from 1973-83, has said that teachers have "historically been collectively employed domestic servants...,an extension of the family...whose role in life was to perpetuate traditional values in the younger generation and to house break kids so they would be equipped to carry out the traditions of their forebears" (Herndon, 1983, p. 17). Although Mr. Herndon may not be the most neutral of observers, the evidence is clear that teachers have been reprimanded, suspended, dismissed, fined, and even jailed for real and imagined violations of public standards. Interestingly, John Scopes was in trouble for going dancing on weekends prior to being fired for teaching Darwinism (Thomas, et al., 1991, p. 171).

By the 1950's, dismissal of teachers based on their private conduct had decreased. By the 1970's, teachers had begun to challenge unreasonable dismissals with increasing frequency (Thomas, et al., 1991). The enactment of tenure laws to protect teachers from arbitrariness on the part of school boards along with the advent of collective bargaining greatly impacted teacher dismissals. Certainty in determining the impact of tenure alone or collective bargaining alone, is impossible, since they simply do not exist alone. One way, however, to study the evolution of teaching, is to analyze court cases involving teachers, to determine how the profession is viewed by the courts. Although courts operate in a world apart from education, they do not operate in a vacuum apart from society.

Employment relationships have evolved over time to reflect an evolving society. So too, have laws been enacted that reflect these changes. The change in the employment relationship that is the focus of this study is the change required because of the initiation of the practice of collective bargaining. Collective bargaining is defined as "a system of labor-management relations to determine wages, hours, and other conditions of employment" (Dilts & Walsh, 1988, p. 3). Teachers, like other workers, collectively organized in order that they might speak with one voice, in the hope that one collective voice might improve their lot.

When congress enacted the National Labor Relations Act in 1935, it exempted public employers -- governments and their agencies -- from the obligation to engage in collective bargaining (97 Harvard Law Review, p. 1676, May 1984). As of 1935, it was seen as socially desirable and morally correct that labor (private-sector labor) be freely allowed to present its views to managment, and to have an effective voice concerning the terms and conditions of employment (Dilts &

Walsh, 1988). Because no statute dominates public sector organizing in the way the National Labor Relations Act (NLRA) governs private sector organizing, it is impossible to set out "most of the law" of public sector organizing singly (Leibig, 1987; Valente, 1994). Until the 1960's arguments against allowing public employees bargaining rights carried the day.   Although many specific reservations were expressed concerning public-sector bargaining, for the purposes of this study, these reservations can all be encompassed within the broad assumption that granting public employees bargaining rights would endanger the public good (97 Harvard Law Review, p. 1676).

In 1947, Congress amended the 1935 National Labor Relations Act, exempting public employers from coverage, within the provisions of the Taft-Hartley Act.   Section 2.(2) of the Taft-Hartley Act implicitedly recognizes the theory that Congress may not pass statutes governing state and local employer-employee relations (Dilts & Walsh, 1988).   The individual states were left to decide whether to allow public-sector bargaining, and in what form. By the 1960's, as public employee organizations grew in number and in strength, and as society grew more militant and more tolerant simultaneously, Congress and several states enacted laws granting bargaining rights to public employees. William Gould (1986), among others, viewed this change as the consequence of several factors: the turmoil of the 1960's, a perceived gap between benefits in the public and private sectors, and increased attention to the public sector by a trade-union movement in search of arenas in which it could recoup its membership losses among private employees.

Teachers, like other public employees, traditionally had negligible input into the conditions under which they worked. In the 1960's, however, teachers, spurred on by the success of the United Federation of Teachers in New York City, sought bargaining rights (Strahan & Turner, 1987). Today, collective bargaining in some form is a reality for public employees of the federal government and most state governments (97 Harvard L. Rev., p. 1679). Most states have enacted a variety of laws covering public employees, ranging from simple "meet and confer" requirements to comprehensive statutes (Blackburn, 1977, p. 27).   Only ten states do not have legislation protecting public-sector bargaining rights, (Arizona, Arkansas, Colorado, Louisiana, Mississippi, North Carolina, South Carolina, Utah, Virginia, and West Virginia), (Dilts, Boyda, Sherr, 1993, p. 260).

Evolution of Public Sector Bargaining

A significant difference between public sector bargaining and private sector bargaining, and a major reason that public sector bargaining tends to be more difficult for the public to fully accept, is the impact upon a greater percentage of the public that public sector bargaining implies. There is often relatively little interest in the negotiations in a given industry, beyond the immediate families of managment, workers, and perhaps shareholders. In contrast, the public schools have a direct impact on most citizens by the taxes they pay, and the education they provide their youth. Whenever people's taxes might be affected by collective bargaining, there are many more potential objectors to the form that any negotiations might take. In the perception of some citizen groups there has been a reallocation of funds for the primary benefit of union membership (Ostrander, 1987). Some observers, notably (Doherty, 1979; Seeley, 1979; Ostrander, 1987), have made the assertion that members of the public have begun to associate collective bargaining with the decline in test scores and the "quality of educational programs." Whether or not there is a causal connection, those within the public schools have long been aware that their actions impact the community at large, and negotiations that "public" employees engage in will quite legitimately be closely scrutinized by the community.

The differences between public and private sector bargaining are debatable and continually evolving. These arguments range from the view that the different economics between the two sectors makes similar treatment inappropriate, to the fact that less differentiation in the public sector between supervisory and other employees, would make bargaining more difficult. The most frequently cited difference is that unions in the public sector can bring pressure on their employers through the political process (Gould, 1986). This distinction is only in degree, for although public sector unions may arguably use politics more frequently, private sector unions are also deeply involved in the political process (Gould, p. 177).

Public sector labor relations is inherently political. The purposes of labor organizations (to enable employees to participate in work-related decisions) and the means of labor organizations (collectivizing workers, lobbying elected and appointed officials, influencing public opinion, and engaging in collective bargaining) are highly political in nature (Love & Sulzner, 1972; Kearney, 1984).

Collective bargaining itself is highly political, as it operates as a system of governance determining the functions of the workplace (Kearney, p. 79).

In 1959, Wisconsin became the first state to enact legislation allowing collective bargaining in the public sector, for municipal employees (Thomas, et al., 1991). The Wisconsin legislature then formally granted state employees bargaining rights in 1966 (Weisberger, 1977). Under that act (known as the State Employment Labor Relations Act or SELRA) the scope of bargaining was exceedingly narrow (Weisberger, p. 700). After Wisconsin, federal action followed in 1962 when President Kennedy extended organizational and collective bargaining rights to federal employees. [Exec. Order No. 10,988, 3 C.F.R. 521 (1959-63 Compilation)], revoked, Exec. Order No. 11, 491, 3 C.F.R. 254 (1974), 5 U.S.C. section 7301 (1970).

Presently, around 40 states have legislation authorizing collective bargaining for public employees, generally (Sharp, 1992; O'Reilly, 1992). 41 states, as of 1989, have laws permitting boards of education to engage in collective bargaining with teacher organizations (Fischer, et al., 1991). Only Mississippi, North Carolina, Texas, and Virginia specifically prohibit collective bargaining for all public school employees (Fischer, et al., p. 41). 45 states have legislation requiring school districts either to "meet and confer" or bargain collectively with employee unions (Keith & Girling, 1991).

Some states have no laws concerning collective bargaining; to the extent that there is any regulation it is by common law (for these purposes "common law" means interpretations by judges that establish precedent, in contrast to actual legislation). Even in states lacking statutes authorizing public bargaining, however, collective negotiation is often accepted in practice (Dilts, Boyda, Sherr, 1993). Even in North Carolina, where formal collective bargaining for public employees is illegal, an informal process of discussions between management and labor, similar to "meet and confer" practices exist (Rhodes & Brown, 1992).

Because of the constitutional right to free assembly, teachers have the right to join professional associations. This right, however, does not necessarily allow for teachers to bargain collectively with school boards. Teachers' associations are bound by state statute in states where legislation exists governing bargaining in the public sector (Dilts, et al., p. 209). Some states allow teacher-board negotiations, some states demand teacher-board negotiations, and some states prohibit recognition of collective agreements between teachers and boards. Where no state statute exists, local school boards generally have the discretion to bargain with teachers' associations (Dilts, et al., p. 212).

The contracts between teachers and their employers define, or attempt to define, the obligations, responsibilities, and legal rights of both parties to the contract. It is with that knowledge that the quest begins for a greater understanding of unionization in education.

Attempting to assess the impact of unions upon teachers has been done before, most often in assessments of salary differences between union and non-union districts. A common argument in the public sector collective bargaining literature, and an argument which devalues these studies, is that economic conditions strongly influence collective bargaining outcomes, as well as the structure, tactics, and processes surrounding the collective bargaining relationship (see e.g., Lewin, 1981; Feuille, 1973; Gely, 1993, p. 387). When "times are tough" as most states and school districts claim they are presently, greater scrutiny is given to collective bargaining outcomes. Ironically from the point of view of teachers, and predictably from the point of view of "management" and many citizens, some observers of public sector bargaining have alleged that unions have contributed to, if not caused, state and local fiscal difficulties by inflating payroll costs (Spero & Capozzola, 1973; Kearney, 1984). Collective bargaining's impact on school budgets is, as usual, arguable. Superintendents and Boards had always faced demands for better education at lower cost, so the advent of collective bargaining merely meant the "nuisance of dealing with yet another constituent group" (Osterman, 1985, p. 434).

Chapter 9

Collective Bargaining in Education

A good definition of collective bargaining is "a subtle blend of legal requirement and voluntary contract, of local flexibility and general impact, and of public policy and private accommodation" (Edwards, 1993, p. 77). Most often "collective bargaining refers to the organizing of employees for the purpose of negotiation and administration of a contractual or legally enforceable agreement between the employee and the employer" (Keith & Girling, 1991, p. 285). Others have referred to collective bargaining as "the continuous process in which representatives of the employer and employees meet to jointly establish the terms and conditions of employment for workers in a bargaining unit" (Kearney, 1984, p. 81); or as "a formal relationship which continues over time between labor and management, involving the joint determination of wages and other terms and conditions of employment" (Kearney, 1984, p. 105). The important distinction between actual collective bargaining and "meet and confer" agreements is that collective bargaining involves "mutual or joint" decision-making, while "meet and confer" agreements allow for unilateral decisions to be made by the employer after having "listened" to the employees concerns.

Like the issues of higher teacher pay and better working conditions, how collective bargaining and its consequences have impacted students is very much open to debate, with both sides of the debate voicing strong views. McDonnell and Pascal (1979, p.xiii), noted that "how any of the consequences of collective bargaining influence the rate of learning or other student interests remains largely unknown." Although teachers have claimed to organize for reasons related to improving education services (Jessup, 1978), the effect of bargaining on educational services, programs, and student outcomes has been largely ignored in the research (Goldschmidt & Painter, 1988). Such incomplete and inconclusive research concerning higher pay, better climate, and the impact of collective bargaining on students has been troublesome to teachers seeking higher pay and better working conditions.

Kerchner & Mitchell (1988) make the claim that collective bargaining has contributed to a loss of confidence by the public in the system of school governance, a deemphasis of concern for school effectiveness and productivity, and a trivialization of teacher work. Urban (1991) disputes the conclusions reached by Kerchner & Mitchell. It is Urban's position that although teacher unions can try any number of things to escape a negative image, they cannot escape the "negativism" that the school reform reports (and the media attention that they have received) have created for unions in general, and teachers' unions in particular. The crusade for "reform" has implanted the notion in the minds of large numbers of the public and large numbers of our political leaders that the public schools are deeply in need of fixing (Urban, 1991).

Collective bargaining and the power that came with it, allowed the collective voice of teachers to become a factor in educational policy making. A good contract reduced the possibility of unilateral decision-making by the administration and the school board and gives the teacher union a partnership role in educational policy-making (Cheng, 1981). Good contracts contain a "network of rules," established through the bargaining process, providing substantive guidelines affecting nearly every aspect of the workplace (Eberts & Stone, 1984, p. 13). In the context of the public schools, rules are written that define the rights and duties of teachers to particular assignments, govern the compensation of teachers, establish disciplinary sanctions for failure to comply with certain standards, and to some extent provide for what level of teacher participation will go into governance of the workplace (Eberts & Stone, 1984). Although there has been more "reform" involvement in recent years on the part of teachers' organizations, traditionally their bargaining was confined to narrowly conceived questions of salary and working conditions. Sometimes that narrow focus was due to their own conceptions of self-interest and sometimes it was due to restrictive bargaining legislation (Mitchell, 1989; Firestone & Bader, 1992).

Variability of State Statutes

Most states have enacted statutes governing teachers' bargaining rights, and school boards must negotiate with teachers in accordance with the statutorily prescribed process (McCarthy, 1987). State statutes and restrictions on the scope of bargaining vary, and the application of the statutes may vary even within states from school district to school district (O'Reilly, 1992). The variances in the state laws range from statutory provisions prohibiting collective bargaining, to no statutory provisions, to provisions mandating bargaining and allowing teachers to strike (Taylor & Witney, 1992). State legislatures that prohibit teacher collective bargaining, like Virginia's, fear most the scenario described by Piskulich (1992) in which the de facto power of labor effectively overwhelms de jure legislative authority over the appropriations process.

Most states have statutory provisions addressing issues surrounding school employment relations, several states rely on the authority of case law, and a handful of states rely on attorney general opinions (LaMorte, 1992). The predominant characteristic of state bargaining laws and systems is diversity with respect to the scope of negotiations, impasse procedures, unfair labor practices, and enforcement procedures (Nesbitt, 1976; Valente, 1994). Even states that authorize collective bargaining usually exempt from bargaining those terms that are "exclusive management rights" (Valente, 1994, p. 192).

The fact that state statutes vary has been made possible by a determination within the federal courts that constitutional protection is afforded persons to form and be members of a union, but that no constitutional right exists to collectively bargain [See Thomas v. Collins, 323 U.S. 516 (1945) wherein it was held that union membership is protected by the right of association under the First and Fourteenth Amendments]. States, while allowing "unionism," have been quite inconsistent in the extent to which they have made collective bargaining for teachers possible (Ostrander, 1987).

One of the most significant issues facing the public sector is machinery for resolving disputes in the face of prohibitions on the right to strike. Many states have some limited provisions for dispute settlement. Some limit machinery to specific categories of workers (Taylor & Witney, 1992). The need for some type of procedure to settle disputes is often cited within the literature. Taylor & Witney (1992) go so far as to say "it does not make sense to outlaw public employee strikes while failing to provide an effective substitute" (p. 417). Indiana is cited as an example of a state in which strikes by teachers are prohibited but there is no impasse procedure, so in effect, teachers are compelled to accept the final offer of school boards. Because of this situation, teachers often strike in Indiana, despite the legal prohibition since there is no alternative available (Taylor & Witney, 1992). "Prohibitions and penalties do not, of course, prevent strikes. They simply raise the cost to the strikers" (Stieber, 1973).

Prior research suggests that public-sector bargaining is so decentralized because of a lack of product market competition and a reluctance on the part of officials to relinquish political autonomy and decision-making power (Lewin and McCormick, 1981, as cited in Gely & Chandler, 1993, p. 381). Because of the wide variance, court decisions based on interpretations of the language of a particular state's collective bargaining act and the language of a specific school district's contract, may or may not be controlling within a given jurisdiction, let alone outside a given jurisdiction. Whatever might be the value of consistency and uniformity among the states, that value has been outweighed by Congress' intent to leave these matters to the individual states. Therefore, the rights of workers vary considerably from state to state, and often within states based on the category of the worker. Our present political environment in which more and more state power as a result of less federal "interference" is continually sought does not bode well for national legislation in any form.

State legislatures and consequently, legislation, is a product of the political and sociological environment of a given state, and it is no secret that many differences exist between the states. Since enactment of new legislation often follows social pressure, and the articulation of a need by a certain social group, there exist great differences among the state legislatures as reflected by the social differences among the states. A study of the history of particular states' legislation concerning public sector bargaining is not this study's focus, however, the reader should be advised that the differences between collective bargaining laws in states such as New York and Wyoming, or Iowa and Virginia, is largely due to the tremendous cultural differences between the states, and the consequent pressures put upon their legislatures.

Because of the differences in labor laws, as well as the absence of such laws in certain states, major differences exist in bargaining rights and practices (McCarthy, 1987). In many states, statutes limit the scope of bargaining, directly affecting wages, hours, and working conditions. Consequently, in education, the NEA and the AFT lobby to affect the outcome of those laws. Public sector unions, and specifically the NEA and AFT tend to lobby, engage in political activities, public relations activities, and indeed litigate cases that may not be clearly linked to a specific problem in the bargaining unit at that time (Jascourt, 1993).

A few states, such as New York, have a detailed, comprehensive collective bargaining statute. In contrast, Virginia and North Carolina prohibit negotiated contracts between teachers' organizations and school boards (McCarthy, 1987). North Carolina has the most prohibitive legislation related to public sector bargaining of any state (Rhodes & Brown, 1992). In Kentucky, even though there is no specific enabling statute, the Kentucky Supreme Court has ruled that a public employer may recognize an employee organization for the purpose of collective bargaining [Board of Trustees of Univ. of Kentucky v. Public Employees Council No. 51, American Federation of State, County, and Mun. Employees, 571 S.W.2d 616 (Ky. 1978)]. Since individual state legislation, and/or court decisions control bargaining rights, generalizations do not come easily in this field. Just as there is considerable disagreement over bargaining rights, there is also great disagreement over what subjects may be negotiable.

Traditional models of the public sector labor relations system, show a variety of inputs influencing the behavior of management, labor, and the agencies charged with regulation of the system. The players have roughly the same "power" in the bargaining relationship (Rhodes & Brown, 1992). In North Carolina and Virginia, as a means of contrast, the critical system input is the political culture that includes strong anti-union attitudes (Rhodes & Brown, 1992). Management is free to dictate the terms of employment unilaterally.

Perhaps not surprisingly, the states without collective bargaining legislation are usually southern or western. These states have consistently been more resistant to change, perhaps best illustrated by their almost universal reluctance to the granting of civil rights. Another common bond among these states has been their almost universal support for Republican presidential candidates in the years since public-sector collective bargaining has existed. Georgia's backing of "native-son" Carter in 1976 and 1980, and Arkansas' support for "native-son" Clinton in 1992 notwithstanding. The "linkage," both real and perceived, of unions with the Democratic party fits the voting results for states without historic fondness for organized labor. Generally, the less affluent, less industrialized southern states have not been known for policy innovations, and that pattern is borne out in collective bargaining legislation (Kearney, 1984). In states that do not permit formal negotiations with public workers, the policy of no labor relations policy appears to be a conscious choice of state lawmakers in their quest to provide "good business climates" for their states by holding down public employee compensation (Kearney, 1984, p. 60).

"The Evolution of Collective Bargaining"

Like teaching, law, and most every other element in our society, collective bargaining has gone through an evolutionary process that has resulted in today's bargaining structure. The historical interpretation of bargaining is, like most historical interpretations, open to some debate, with some historians viewing its evolution differently from others. Most, however, believe that collective bargaining in its earliest form predates the constitution (Dilts & Walsh, 1988, p. 4). Despite its existence, collective bargaining was left out of the constitution, just as education was. There exists therefore, no constitutional right to bargain, nor constitutional prohibition against it.

This work refers to collective bargaining as the term is commonly used, however, it should be noted that teacher's associations, and the NEA in particular, often prefer the term "professional negotiations." Whatever we refer to collective bargaining as, the mechanism of bargaining and the concept of professionalism are compatible, at least from the perspective of most teachers (Webster, 1985, p. 33). Although many people did and still do consider collective bargaining "unprofessional," teachers are faced with the dilemma of needing collective action to have any impact on gaining greater autonomy in their workplace, one of the "requirements" of professionalism.

Collective bargaining is essentially a power relationship and a process of power accommodation (Perry & Wildman, 1970; Piskulich, 1992). Nyberg (1990) quotes Bertrand Russell (1938, p. 12) who said "the fundamental concept in social science is power." Nyberg believes that two points are drawn from Russell's statement. First, that we can't understand social life, without the concept of power, and second, that "power is morally neutral, it can be used by good and bad people for good and bad reasons in producing good and bad results" (p. 48). The concept of empowerment, discussed earlier, is strongly connected to teacher collective bargaining, as both apparently seek to "improve" the working conditions of teachers.

Whether or not "power" is "morally neutral" as Nyberg proclaims, the perception that one has of collective bargaining and its impact on power relationships, tends, like most things, to mirror the interests of the perceiver. If teachers tend to feel that collective bargaining has increased their power and is therefore "good," school boards often feel that collective bargaining has decreased their power and is therefore "bad."

In The School Board Primer, written as a "guide for school board members," collective bargaining is seen as strictly an "adversarial process with both parties striving for advantage" (Wiles & Bondi, 1985, p. 122). Other authors have similarly referred to collective bargaining as "necessarily adversarial," without commenting on the propriety of bargaining (Keith & Girling, 1991, p. 292). Piskulich (1992) described all public sector collective bargaining as "less an economic relationship than a manifestly political interaction" (p. 6). Still others feel that the adversarial process often means that "negotiations" are accompanied by acrimony and name-calling, which has been "shortsighted and contrary to the best interests of both parties" (Clark, 1981, p. 368). There is a growing concern that the adversarial nature of collective bargaining is, or at least can be, counter-productive to education's goals of achieving genuine shared decision-making as a positive means to solving real problems (Keith & Girling, 1991; Koppich, 1993).

The power sought by teachers may be in achieving greater control over the decision-making process used by management, or simply in seeking better wages and working conditions. "The underlying consideration in collective negotiations is participation in the decision-making process, which is a natural extension of our democratic lifestyle" (Rebore, 1984, p. 247).

Teachers have been among the most militant public employees (Levine & Hagburg, 1979). In public employment, teachers' organizations have been leaders in organized labor's fight to open up the range of bargainable issues to include almost every conceivable item that would even remotely affect their terms and conditions of employment (Metzler, 1973). The range of negotiable issues is critical to the status actually possessed by the "employees" at the bargaining table (Piskulich, 1992). Educators see it as being in the public's as well as their own interest to be able to negotiate on as many topics as possible, including topics that school boards have traditionally seen as policy (Ostrander, 1987). The rationale from the point of view of the teachers is that as "experts" in the field, based on their special training and expertise, they are able to effectively consider the implications upon the students of a mulititude of potential bargaining issues. Whether such increases in bargaining topics beyond the old traditional "wages, hours, and working conditions" is positive or negative seems to depend primarily, as usual, upon whose side one is on.

The literature generally speaks of the natural evolution of the workplace in society and the inevitability of public sector bargaining. It was surprising to some, not that collective bargaining for teachers became commonplace, but that teachers allowed themselves to be under authoritarian rule by superintendents and principals, decades after such rule disappeared from much of industry (Genck, 1991). However appropriate or inappropriate one might view the shift in the power structure toward teachers, power can only be exerted by a party if that party provides a service which others depend upon. Mutual interdependence must exist for bargaining to be possible. If a party is dependent upon another for survival, then bargaining cannot exist, beyond any goodwill that the stronger party bestows upon the weaker party. For negotiations to take place there are two essential requirements: (a) the parties must be, legally or otherwise, "equals" and (b) each party must be able to utilize pressure to induce the other to compromise (Metzler, 1973, p. 141).

From the literature on bargaining, it is abundantly clear that good bargaining is an art. An art that is entirely dependent upon the situation of the parties. "The policies agreed upon by unions and managements fundamentally reflect the more enduring features of the environment of the collective bargaining relationship" (Gerhart,1976, p. 331). In other words, like so much of life, the circumstances surrounding the bargaining control the ultimate product of the bargaining relationship. In districts with ample funds, bargaining tends to be less adversarial than in districts with limited resources. Such simple truths are critical to an understanding of any bargaining relationship.

Collective Bargaining's Impact

As addressed earlier in this study, the impact of collective bargaining on student outcomes is largely unknown. Those studies that have attempted to assess the impact of bargaining on student outcomes, have found very little difference in the average quality of education between union and nonunion districts (Eberts & Stone, 1984). Although both proponents and opponents of unionism are "certain" that their cause positively impacts students, the consequences of collective bargaining upon student outcomes is not readily apparent (Eberts & Stone, 1984, p. 42).

The research on the impact of collective bargaining on how schools have been run is more conclusive. "Teachers covered by collective bargaining agreements, as compared with teachers not covered, receive higher salaries, teach smaller classes, and spend slightly less time instructing students but more time preparing for classes" (Eberts & Stone, 1984, p. 173). The positive effect that bargaining has on teacher salaries is small (Cooper, 1982; Cresswell & Spargo, 1980; Finch & Nagle, 1984; Lipsky, 1982). The major difference then between nonunion and union districts was in the cost of education: for the same level of educational quality, the annual operating costs per pupil in union districts is 15 percent higher than in similar nonunion districts (Eberts & Stone, 1984, p. 173).

A system that has been shown to increase the cost of education, without any correlating increase in the "results," however subjective, can be and often is the target of much criticism. For every advocate of collective bargaining, there seems to be a staunch opponent of teacher unionism, declaring that teachers have lost their sense of duty and professionalism and have lost sight of the goals of education (Eberts & Stone, 1984). Some members of the public feel that collective bargaining has diverted the attention of teachers away from the classroom and into the bargaining room, to the detriment of the student (Eberts & Stone, 1984). When teachers unionize, they are perceived by some to switch from the role of a dedicated classroom teacher to that of a dedicated union member (Eberts & Stone, 1984). Lortie has referred to the "ritual pity" that teachers have historically received as poorly paid, "dedicated" workers, who were subsequently exempted from high performance expectations and rigorous public scrutiny (Lortie, 1975, p. 221). Such a relationship might very well change, given increased teacher aggressiveness (Lortie, p. 221).

Another criticism of unions and/or collective bargaining lies in the "threat to efficiency" that unions often represent, validly or not. "Unions tend to resist or seek compensation for changes proposed or instituted by management in the interests of efficiency; innovation and change are often perceived as threats to stability and security" (Perry & Wildman, 1970, p. 223).

Some of the harshest critics have even blurred the distinction between unions and professional associations in their commentaries.

The NEA is probably the most intellectually dishonest organization in America. It is part union, part professional organization, and part political party. Its object is to control the Congress, the fifty state legislatures, the Democratic Party, the curriculum in all the schools, public and private, and the entire teaching profession. Its interest in academics is subordinate to its radical political and social ends (Blumenfeld, 1984, p. 139).

One person's "radical," however, is another's "reasonable person" as Herndon illustrates in a 1977 address: "What then of increasing unionization and militancy among public employees? It's simple. Spurn a moderate and create a militant. The price of stability is equity. Deny equity and induce instability" (Herndon, 1983, p. 84).

The opposition to the NEA's influence was predominantly conservative, as the "conservatives" never forgave the organization for endorsing former President Carter in 1976. That first ever national endorsement labeled the NEA as "Democratic," and conservatives have since openly opposed the NEA, despite its "power." Beyond written criticisms, conservative groups mobilized supporters and raised money to spread their gospel of anti-NEA sentiments. A grassroots lobby called Save Our Schools was begun in 1980 by Dan C. Alexander, Jr., and among other things, their official "Newsletter" stated that "the NEA Teacher Union is a threat to traditional moral values and educational standards of the United States" (Save Our Schools," Newsletter, May 1985, p. 7, from Berube, 1988, p. 9). Mr. Alexander's characterizations of the NEA included such musings as: "the NEA is a militant teacher union dominated and run by a hard core group of radical educators.," and "the NEA is run by an ultra-liberal group of educators who are more interested in changing America's values and politics than educating her children" (Berube, 1988, p. 10). The 1992 presidential election was not the first time those on the political right have used "family values," to castigate "liberal, pro-union," persons.

In The Decline and Fall of American Education, union membership is considered a "major factor in the decline of student performance" (Salser & West, 1991, p.164). In that same work, the NEA is described as a "gigantic labor union," in which "professionalism, sacrifice, and dedication" could not be "further from the truth" (Salser & West, p. 165). Salser, it should be noted, was a former member of President Reagan's National Council on Educational Research, which quite clearly identifies the type of "research" that Reagan received concerning the NEA and teachers. Salser and West blame unions for numerous "obvious" effects including intimidating school boards, administrators, parents, businesses, and even children. "Unionism in education poses many dangers; but the greatest basic danger is this: Power-hungry unions are interested in power, money, and leverage; they are not interested in students or the taxpayers for whom they supposedly work" (Salser & West, p. 167). The politics of Reagan and Bush were decidedly not pro-union, whether the union represented air traffic controllers or teachers, and in such a context, the defensiveness of the teachers' associations in the 1980's may have been well placed. Other commentators have taken a different view. In a book published by the NEA, Allan A. Glatthorn (1992, p. 16), states that "both the NEA and the AFT have played an active role in advancing the agenda for school improvement." "Better education...is and should be the goal of educators and their unions. To that end, collective bargaining has been and will continue to be an integral part of the process" (Poltrock & Goss, 1993, p. 182).

The NEA responded to many of the attacks, and characterized the attackers as "extremists" (Berube, 1988, p. 11). Whatever the merits of either side, the NEA had now taken its place in the minds of most within the spectrum of American politics. To some, such political involvement was "unprofessional," to others it was a requirement of "good citizenship." Whether the NEA's involvement was good or bad, tended not surprisingly to depend upon one's level of agreement with the "politics" of the organization. In much the same manner as whether the NEA particularly, and the AFT to a lesser extent, were seen as "unions" by their critics and as "professional associations," by their supporters.

The change in the political activity of the NEA has been dramatic. In 1956, the NEA research division conducted a membership poll asking whether members should participate in politics. Only 25%

said yes (Berube, 1988, p. 18). In 1975, a similar poll of the NEA representative assembly, over 92% supported the endorsement of Jimmy Carter as the presidential candidate (Berube, p. 18). According to some, the reasons for the increasing politicization of the NEA were the rise of teacher unionism in the 1960's and the emergence of the militancy of the civil rights movement. As a result, as NEA affiliates won collective bargaining victories, they also became aware of the potential benefits of political involvement (Berube, p. 18). The downside to open political involvement is the alienation of some members. After all, not all NEA members voted for Jimmy Carter, despite their organization's endorsement. The potential for divisiveness when open support and opposition to national candidates is at issue, is great. Philip W. Jackson (1987, p. 56) discusses the future of teaching as a balance between conservative and liberal outlooks that educators seek in order to curry favor with both sides. However one views the "politics" of the teachers' associations, the NEA and the AFT have shaped federal school aid policies, have leveraged appropriations for favored programs from Congress, have blocked proposals (such as tuition tax credits) that they hated, and have acquired genuine power within the Republican and Democratic Parties (though steadily less within the Republican party), and their support is usually eagerly sought by candidates (Finn, 1985).

If there has been a true "degradation of labor" as Michael Apple writes (1987, p. 73), then teachers need to feel threatened by attacks on any segment of labor, and should perhaps join forces in organized action with nurses, social workers, and clerical workers, who are in similar positions within society. These professions tend to receive relatively low pay, and low status, but are expected to carry great responsibilities.

A Look to the Future

The board of education and the administration are charged with representing the interests of the public. Both the interest in having the best possible education for children and the interest in having that education provided for at the lowest possible cost are legitimate (Walter, 1975). The dilemma arises in the view of many, that the "best possible education," and "lowest possible cost" are mutually exclusive terms.

Teachers, as professionals, also spend a large percentage of their time in school performing rather "unprofessional" tasks. Taxpayers might be better off if teachers were allowed to focus on teaching, and paraprofessionals were hired and paid to supervise lunch, hallways, playgrounds, run copying machines, and perform other tasks for which a qualified teacher is unnecessary (Maeroff, 1988). Between 10 and 50 percent of a teacher's time is spent on noninstructional duties - recording test scores, monitoring the halls, and so forth (Carnegie Forum, 1986, p. 15). Society would not consider paying doctors or lawyers their hourly rates to have them do photocopying, nor would most doctors or lawyers consider performing those tasks an efficient way in which to spend their work time. Perhaps, we should consider why teachers should be expected to do many such tasks when other lower paid, less qualified individuals can do the work. If teachers could spend more time teaching, and teaching was deemed more valuable, then perhaps salaries might be raised to more appropriately reflect that value. Today, since the teacher makes little more than the secretary, there is no great need seen to lessen the non-teaching duties of teachers.

Teachers, independently and through their associations, have apparently not done a tremendous job of convincing the public at large of the value of their service. Or alternatively, the public sees little value in changing a salary structure which seems to allow for decent, and occasionally excellent public education at relatively low cost.

Whether "professional unionism" (Koppich, 1993) can take hold, and whether the concept is actually any different from the present situation, is open for debate. The concept as described "joint custody of reform, union-management collaboration, and concern for the public interest" (Koppich, p. 194) is difficult to fault. Whether the concept can have any real impact on schools, or if it is merely a debate about words, is unknown.

The variation in public sector labor policy between and within states substantiates the fact that "disjointed incrementalism" (Braybrooke and Lindblom, 1963; Piskulich, 1992) is the dominant decision-making strategy at work in this sphere. Piskulich (1992) describes public sector labor policy as "a varied patchwork of provisions, a series of experiments lying on a continuum of mandated collective bargaining to outright prohibition"(p. 15).

To many, the consequences of state by state bargaining are illogical and inequitable (Herndon, 1983; Levine and Hagburg, 1979). Others have actually predicted that the legal framework will be "rationalized" to impose some form of national labor law for the public sector as is present in the private sector's NLRA (Weber, 1979;

Maguire, 1979). Taylor & Witney (1992, p. 426) contend that if organized labor would be "socially responsible" and management would accept in good faith the principle of collective bargaining, the reliance upon law to enforce a viable and responsible collective bargaining system would decrease...leading to the end of the adversarial relationship between management and unions, and to a program of genuine cooperation and mutual accommodation. Nevertheless, the reality of the situation seems to be that any national scheme for teacher collective bargaining is present only in a far off Utopia. It is the goal of this study then, to analyze teacher dismissals within a given setting, in order to ultimately, compare and contrast the cases, and reach reasoned conclusions concerning the impact of unions/associations within and among these jurisdictions. Within the complex and controversial issue of professionalism, and its implications for teacher collective bargaining as a background and framework, this study will look to selected jurisdictions individually. These jurisdictions will attempt to portray three different points "or experiments" as Piskulich (1992) has referred to them, along the continuum that is public sector bargaining.

Society's Expectations

Our society has burdened schools with high expectations (Cuban, 1989), that may in themselves indicate a certain level of professionalism is inherent in teaching. Such high expectations would surely not be placed upon persons with less than professional standing. When the nation considered itself threatened by the early success of the Soviet space program during the cold war, we passed the National Defense Education Act and called on the schools to stress science and mathematics (Nystrand, 1992). In the 1960's, our public schools were given the role of social reformer, by our need to integrate. In a society that was largely nonintegrated in housing and employment, the schools were to integrate education, with the hope that out of the classroom would come the model relations for the rest of society. The schools were seen as the place in which America could begin to cope with its two most difficult problems: race and poverty (Tyler, 1976, p. 18).

Many consider the schools to be a tremendous vehicle for social change; others maintain that education can also act as an impediment to social change (Brookover & Erickson, 1975, p. 66). "Schools that are designed to teach the traditional attitudes and beliefs which maintain the society as it has been are not as likely to produce change as those which are designed to motivate students for the kinds of activities that would be associated with a different future" (Brookover & Erickson, 1975, p. 80). Beyond that, "the concept of education as producing or impeding social change is enormously complicated by the fact that the educational system is itself a part of the society which it is changing" (Brookover & Erickson, 1975, p. 68). Ultimately, for the school to change the social structure there must be considerable change in the economic, political, and every other system. The same is true for the other institutions within society; for the economic and political system to change, there would need to be change within the educational system (Brookover & Erickson, 1975, p. 118).

As society demands more and more from its teachers in particular, and schools in general, it is not overly surprising that those from whom more is expected might naturally tend to see a need to be granted higher standing in order to reflect such apparent value. In order to gain higher standing and a voice in school affairs, educators felt the need, as had their brethren in other industries, to unite in order to form a more powerful coalition.

Brief Summary from the Literature

"The value of good schools is far more important than their cost" (Genck, 1991, p. 165). Whatever else impacts public education, it is the financing of the schools that tells us, whatever the political rhetoric may be, of the value that we as a society place upon education. How to properly pay for education in order to achieve success, and possibly even some degree of equity, is an issue that drives all else within the realm of public education.

Given the importance of teacher professionalization to the current reform agenda, it should be of value to consider what impact recent court decisions have had upon the "professionalization" of teachers. Since an appeal to most taxpayers concerning the long-term benefit of worthy social progress and increased international competitiveness, falls upon either deaf or non-listening ears, teachers might need to alter their arguments for higher salaries. If higher salaries simply aren't politically feasible, for a variety of reasons, at least paying attention to people and recognizing their achievements may make them feel more valuable (Maeroff, 1988).

Whether one's values support greater or lesser spending on education, the public does support, through its tax dollars, whatever level of spending is set. Public education is believed generally to have a public relations problem (First, 1992). Much of that problem, comes from the fact that seventy-eight percent of adults have no direct tie to public schools (Bakalis, 1985). Despite such an obstacle, teachers and teachers' organizations might consider improving their public relations skills as a group in order to better persuade the public of the value of spending more money on education. A more successful argument for higher pay might focus on the implications of good schools vs. bad schools and their effect upon property values and future cost control.

Difficulty arises whenever public employees seek greater pay, and particularly so when teachers are the public employees. The commitment of a public school is, or should be, to maximize student outcomes as efficiently as is possible. Public schools then, have a social and a moral commitment to both the patrons, who are compelled to support them, and to the students, who are compelled to attend them (Imber & Neidt, 1990).

Under the philosophical commitments to citizens and students, lies the reality of school budgets which are dominated by fixed costs that allow flexibility for cost reduction in only three areas: educational programming, personnel, and facilities (Wiles & Bondi, 1985). Beyond the expenditures of buildings, insurance, utilities, and peripheral employees, it is teachers who receive the majority of tax money spent. Despite this, it is teachers who, quite frequently and probably quite validly, complain about their low pay with ever increasing intensity. How then may we reconcile the need for an increase in teacher prestige and salary within a society which finds the public schools ever more disappointing, and ever less worthy of their financial support?

Because of the "cost" of teachers, current reform movements within the literature, in order to achieve any level of success, must consider teachers to be at the center of school improvement or school decline. Teachers, like other members of society have evolved over time and have responded to society's demands. Teachers have increased their social significance (if not their social status) and they have been required to specialize within the occupation, and accumulate professional knowledge in order to effectively perform the services expected of them (Bergen, 1992). Despite such evolution, teachers' place and status within our culture has not significantly risen.

Americans seem to have a great ability to distinguish between their interests and the interests of others. "There is a kind of widespread schizophrenia in which people seem, on the one hand, to acknowledge that we have a grave country-wide education problem but also seem, on the other hand, to be reasonably content with their own and their children's education and with their local schools" (Finn & Rebarber, 1992, introduction p. 12; Finn, 1991, p. 98). Beyond education, we see the same logic with regard to our public officials. Nearly everyone feels that Congress needs reform, and that most Congresspersons don't always act in our country's best interests. However, we keep reelecting our incumbents by astonishing numbers and in some instances by astonishing margins.

It is all too easy to see that such beliefs are not fertile ground for radical or even incremental change, so most reform initiatives remain in the minds of their creators, and not within the consensus of the people. The apparent inability to focus beyond the immediate needs of ourselves, and perhaps our community, has been reinforced by the rhetoric of American education and education "reform" that is filled with paeans to the virtues of local control of the schools (Graham, 1992). The absence of educational leadership from Washington, especially during the 1980's, has intensified many of the problems schools face. "There is plenty of room for state and local initiative in educational reform, but the fundamental problems of poverty, single-parent families, inadequate child care, and hopelessness that affect many of our children are in the domain of the country as a whole, not of a beleaguered town with an inadequate tax base" (Graham, p. 77). "The most obvious outcome of these fundamental social changes, as far as the school administrator is concerned, is the lessening or even breakdown of social consensus" (Holmes & Wynne, 1989, p. 160).

American education is vast, decentralized, ponderous, and slow to change (Finn, 1991). At the same time, "change is constant and accelerating and the most striking characteristic of the world we live in and education has not yet recognized this fact" (Postman & Weingartner, 1969, introduction p. xiii). These words written nearly 25 years ago support my underlying premise, that school reform of any sort is easily discussed, but not so easily enacted. Given these circumstances, the ability of teachers to increase their status, and more broadly, for education to make fundamental changes, is in grave doubt.

Different situations require different treatments, and unfortunately for both students and teachers, today's reform efforts often employ terms such as "input-output,""predictability," and "cost-effectiveness"(Giroux, 1988, p. 1), in order to focus on relatively simple solutions to complex problems.   "Conceptually, the reform reports reflect and help perpetuate a technocratic rationality that is at odds with the goals of quality teaching and teachers as reflective practitioners" (Cornbleth, 1989, p. 19).

By putting resources where they can be used, whether to attract more and "better" qualified teachers, or to help achieve more equity for poorly funded schools, the money that is available can gain more results.   If and when more "results" are obtained, more support for public schools will be forthcoming.   If collective bargaining and teacher "unionism" are shown to bear little relationship with teacher dismissals, and the evidence will show that "poor" teachers can be and are dismissed, then perhaps another reason for the public's lack of confidence in the public schools can be discredited.

If any one thing is perfectly clear from a study of the professionalism literature, it is that professionalism is an extremely vague concept that does not lend itself to precise definition. Although it has been a goal of this study to provide definitions that are more valuable than "mere" dictionary definitions, in the case of professionalism, as you will see in the literature review, the best definition of professionalism is dependant upon the context and the opinion of the person doing the defining. Webster's New Collegiate Dictionary defines professionalism as "the conduct, aims, or qualities that characterize or mark a profession or a professional person." So in order to define professionalism, it is necessary to define the professions and professional persons. In other words, professionalism is essentially dependant upon what a given person sees as the "conducts, aims, or qualities" of a profession or a professional.

It is a common feature of our society for persons to expect "professionalism" in the actions of others, whether or not the activities of the other are within the constraints, however vague, of a "profession." Likewise, it is common to aspire to "professionalism," even though there is little consensus upon what "professionalism" is.   Since this study will support the view that the "reform" literature is mostly about "professionalism," the importance of the term "professionalism" is too great to allow for a definition that unfairly confines the broad usage of the term within the literature and within our perceptions.

Overview of Education within the Legal System

The United States has no national system of education. In fact, the Constitution is silent on the matter; however, under the Tenth Amendment, education is considered to be among the powers reserved by the states. The U.S. Supreme Court has repeatedly held that the federal courts may interfere with the actions of state and local officials only when such actions somehow threaten a personal liberty or property right protected by the Constitution or violate federal law (Fischer, Schimmel, Kelly, 1991). All 50 states provide for public education within their state constitutions. Historically, the states have delegated much of their power to local governments. The degree of authority that local school systems have over educational matters depends on a state's constitutional and statutory provisions. How much control the locals actually have is debatable and is in fact different in different states. Although it is the prevailing belief that public schools are controlled locally, many argue that often the state has more meaningful power over education policy than the locals (LaMorte, 1992).

Popkewitz (1987) states: "our world is continually offered as one of ready-made customs, traditions, and order in the things of daily life. Yet the natural order is not natural or inevitable, but constructed historically, socially, and politically" (p. 27). Without some understanding of how behaviors are structured within culture and social interests, our attempts to "reform" schools and our attempts to "reform" teachers and teaching, are an exercise in futility.

What's missing from the school reform debate, is much discussion about money for any new programs and/or reforms, and about the impact of changes on those at the bottom of the economic scale in this country. "Undoubtedly, the law of diminishing returns applies in education. A point could be reached where spending more money on schools would be unproductive, but few if any school districts have ever approached that point" (Seldon, 1985, p. 233). Sizer (1992) states "Getting the people behind the public schools" is not just the politics of annual budgets and bond issues. "It is about living the values which school stands for, whatever one's age"(p. 27). Undertaking the reforms that political leaders espouse requires not only careful attendance to the agenda, but concern about the "silences" that mask aspects of our culture which must be accounted for if true reform is to take hold and flourish (Sizer, 1992).

   To promote the greatest opportunity for learning, we need to strive for decent facilities, and well-paid, well respected teachers. Money alone, however, is not the answer. The answer lies in a radically altered way in which our government views its role in educating our youth, and not coincidentally, the way our government views its role in general. If we continually berate the public schools to the point of suggesting, as former Presidents Reagan and Bush did, that parents receive government aid to remove their children from public schools, then what is the message being sent to those left behind? It took many years for the public schools to deteriorate (assuming that they actually have), and thus, we might expect it to take years for the schools to improve radically. Barzun (1991) found plenty of blame for each side of the political fence when he described the "collapse of the American public school" as coming after "thirty years of blindness on one side and defensive lying on the other" (p. 96).

   The only true hope of making education better for more of us, is to rally behind public education, not abandon all hope. "If a significant number of Americans abandon public education -- either out of lethargy or by opting for private religious, ethnic, or elite academies -- we risk turning public schools into schools of last resort" (Meier, 1995, p. 5). "Schools can squelch intelligence, they can foster intolerance and disrespect, they affect the way we see ourselves in the pecking order. But that's precisely why we cannot abandon our public responsibility to all children, why we need a greater not a lesser commitment to public education" (Meier, 1995, p. 6).   The "individualism" so prevalent in the 1980's is precisely what led to the conclusion that public schools were a "lost cause" and rather than focusing our efforts to improve them, we wasted valuable time debating the merits of different "reforms" or in debating the merits of programs such as the voucher plans which would supposedly allow parents to more easily opt out of the public schools. "It is ludicrous for society to expect public schools by themselves to solve fundamental social problems...nonetheless, education in general, and schools, in particular, can...make important substantive contributions to the problems of society" (Graham, 1992, p. 13).

   Morris Philipson in the editor's preface to Barzun's (1991) work, described both his own and Barzun's belief that the answers to our school problems are there, known of old. "But we have preferred to ignore them, refused to act on them, pursuing instead a host of false leads and so-called 'innovative methods,' even after it became clear that they led nowhere."

Chapter 10

Conclusions

This study celebrates the interconnections within schools and asserts that denying these interconnections is not realistic. Because of the complexities of these interconnections, collective bargaining for teachers alone will not improve schools, just as prohibiting bargaining alone will not improve schools. Nor will either a greater denial or greater acceptance of bargaining alone destroy schools.

If teaching is to improve, and therefore, if public schools are to improve, teachers' organizations need to quite literally "get it together." They (the AFT and the NEA) have wasted untold effort belittling the other, and then alternately condemning or leaping on the bandwagon of particular "reform" proposals. Nothing real distinguishes one from the other despite their frequent wars about vague concepts and vague words. Ultimately, it will make no difference to students, parents, and to society at large, whether a common teachers' organization is perceived to be a union or a professional association, so long as it focuses on a common goal of bettering educational opportunities for the nation's public school children. After accomplishing that unity, and only after accomplishing that unity, will "good" things like higher salaries and greater prestige have an opportunity to find their way out of the quagmire that is presently "school reform."

Densmore (1987) challenges the conventional wisdom that teachers are professionals or semi-professionals. As it is presently organized, teaching is predominantly characterized by conventionality and passivity, not by professional autonomy or creativity. "Viewing teachers as workers may help us understand teacher acquiescence or ambivalence to the structural conditions within which they occupy a subordinate position" (Densmore, 1987, p. 132). Were teachers to more readily view themselves as workers, rather than professionals, they may be better able to recognize both the sources of troubles schools face and potential means of effective action (Densmore, 1987).

Teachers and their organizations, like other American unions, have done a poor job of convincing the average laborer or the public at large of the value of union membership. Strobel (1993) points out that it is now "quite fashionable" to criticize the unions (p. 189). Although Strobel was concerning himself primarily with private sector unions, his arguments remain true to the plight of teachers in this country. In an article appearing in the September 27, 1993 edition of Newsweek, entitled "Still Fighting Yesterday's Battle," Romaine Worster, an ex-union member, brought forth many of the anti-union sentiments expressed "again" in recent years. In the article, unionism is described as a "lopsided religion...all it has is a devil - management," and as one of "the last bastions of socialism" (p. 12). Whether or not these words have any merit, they accurately describe a sense among many Americans that unions are "unproductive, demoralizing, and undermining to the economy" (p. 12). These words tend to imply that "we the people" have catered to the workers for too long.

In contrast, Strobel (1993) makes a rather persuasive argument that both political parties have catered to "business" for too long. He accuses the Democratic party of trying to out-Republican the Republican party by claiming to be good for labor and good for business. He believes that the Democratic party needs to reclaim its traditional base, that is, those persons who rely primarily on their own labor for income. I would extend the argument to teachers, who need to stop trying to out-professionalize the professions, and return to their base as "workers." Through that realization, they might acquire the power necessary through effective collective action that might enable them to improve, however slightly, their working conditions. Teachers, through one effective national union, can attempt to persuade Americans that in order to "better" the standing of more Americans, investment is needed in people, neighborhoods, and education.

Educators alone cannot correct our educational problems

because these problems are not usually confined to educational institutions (Densmore, 1987, p. 156). It appears obvious to many observers of school systems (Cooper, 1991), that any real effort to include teachers in significant school decision making will require a radical rethinking of the way our schools operate. Given that radical rethinking will be difficult within our acceptance of current school structure, any actual "reform" will require a radical departure from present conditions. Whether that departure takes the form of greater "professionalization" for teachers, or the opposite stance of greater unionization and militancy as "unionism" used to imply, is not yet determined.

This thesis proposes that the best "hope" for teachers and consequently students is the "more unionized, less professionalized" approach. Teachers are in fact different from doctors, lawyers, and other "professionals," and those differences don't require any less "professional" action and/or "professional" acceptance, but those differences do mean less time should be spent on considering the similarities. Teaching is a different input, students are a different output, and schools are different "production centers" than more traditional "businesses." Let us accept the differences and move forward.

Reform must be from the "bottom-up" just as our concerns ought to lie with those now relegated to the bottom level. This study shows, among other things, that the courts do not treat teachers very differently than they have in the past. The courts establish their reasoning and then they follow that reasoning in applying it to future cases. Teachers are still dismissed in a manner more like factory workers than physicians, because our society has not been willing to entrust the future of our children to teachers alone. Whether or not such treatment is appropriate, it is the reality. It is from that reality, as reflected by the cases in this study as they pertain to school reform and professionalism, that change within our schools will gradually take place. So as organizations of persons, the two predominant "professional associations" may call themselves whatever they want, it does not matter. What matters is that they unite to increase their voice as a louder voice of reason in support of bottom-up reform. The organizations' to be effective should serve as "conduits for teachers' contributions to decisions that affected their work" (Bascia, 1994, p. 72).

It is the ultimate conclusion of this study that we have wasted much time and effort looking for a sweeping reform proposal that would "cure" what ails the public schools. National reform will not work in an "industry" where almost every factor that leads toward a young person's success is situational. The contradictions within the literature alone serve as evidence that a single satisfactory proposal is not forthcoming. The differences in the law and the application of the law as shown by the analysis of only three of the fifty states indicate that glaring differences in the realities for teachers are present. Mandating broad and unproven reforms will not widely improve schools or teaching, just as mandating certain sentences for criminals has not improved the crime rate. The interconnections between law and education are numerous, and precedent is valuable to both. Just as the courts' must be careful in making certain that "like" situations are truly "like" situations, education reformers must be careful in making certain that the differences in schools are not glossed over in favor of sweeping reforms. That is, people, schools, legal environments, laws, and the realities of teaching are significantly different in different places, and in order to truly "reform" schooling those differences should not be ignored.

It is common among citizens concerned with their public schools to expect only "good" teachers to be influencing their children. However reasonable such an expectation is, it is fraught with the tension between a teachers' expectation of continued employment and a school district's expectation of being allowed to dismiss unacceptable teachers. Just as much of the "professionalism" literature speaks of "drawing lines," the citizens concerned with their public schools expect the courts to draw reasonable boundaries between a teacher's expectations and a district's expectations. Whenever lines are drawn, a certain arbitrariness is inherent, and there will always be examples of dismissals that arguably did not cross that line into unacceptability, and non-dismissals that did.

Recommendations

1. Merger of the AFT and the NEA in order to raise the standing of the "profession" of teaching, and focus the efforts of teachers.

2. Establish some form of agreement on the terms of greater professionalism for teachers, or alternatively, focus upon collective bargaining as a strength of the "profession," rather than continually

attempt to explain how teachers can bargain and be professional simultaneously. (Recommendation number two may only be advanced if recommendation number one is a reality).

3. Less talk from teachers, administrators, and politicians about "reform" and more concern and talk about specific problems in specific schools. If we want to talk broadly about improving our public schools, we should talk about such things as poverty and unequal school financing in order to more equalize opportunity. If opportunity can be more equalized, then perhaps we can concern ourselves with "excellence" and other slightly less important issues.

Retrospective

In looking back over the course of a lengthy study, one is confronted by ways in which the study might have diverged from the path taken. This study deliberately took a rather abstract view of the entire genre of "reform" literature. This was done in order to assess the "rhetoric of reform" generally through an understanding of the broad differences of opinion within the literature and a presentation of those differences as a way of supporting the thesis that the rhetoric as it stands presently can never go beyond rhetoric and become reality. This study focused intentionally on the broad climate of reform.

This section examines some of the ways in which a different approach within this study or a different study altogether might approach this, or a similar problem. In so doing, there must be an appreciation for the likelihood that no two social science researchers approaching this type of study would do things entirely the same way.

An approach that could have been taken would have been one in which the literature in support of one viewpoint would be examined in detail to either support or refute a hypothesis concerning professionalism. For example, there is a line of reasoning within the literature that stands for the proposition that increasing the autonomy, salaries, and level of respect afforded teachers would lead to better teaching. A study could attempt to use dismissal data as one piece of evidence to support the view that in states in which teachers and teachers' organizations have greater input over working conditions through collective bargaining, teachers are afforded greater respect, at least grudgingly, by the boards who must bargain with them "in good faith." The danger of any such attempt to support abstract concepts such as "good teaching" or "greater respect" through the use of data is in the vagueness of the concepts under study.

To deny the existence of other ways to conduct a similar study, is to deny reality. Among the central tenets of this study is the desire for all of us, and for teachers and their organizations specifically, to stop denying reality. This study is but one piece of evidence that the author hopes might be persuasive. Any actions that might be reasonably taken, as always, should be done in light of a competent analysis of all studied options and desired and possible outcomes. Education generally and learning specifically is more about questioning than "knowing," and any study which allows the reader to discover new questions that might lead to a search for new "answers," has assisted the cause. It was this study's purpose to question the status quo and to question the direction that the "reform" literature has taken education, in the hope that the readers might expand the search for the "truth," through still further questioning. Whether we may ever discover the "truth" is perhaps philosophically impossible, but we may be able to discover what most certainly is not the "truth." Ultimately, the phenomenon of school "reform" as this study assessed it, is at least partially at odds with the realities of teachers specifically, and the larger "real" world surrounding and controlling the actions of the schools generally. Within the broad and almost all-encompassing world of school "reform," there arise many issues beyond the scope of this study, some of which the author has attempted to address. The challenge is to further pursue the phenomenon by further questioning its assumptions and its proposals. To do so is to ultimately improve the assumptions and the proposals and perhaps place them more in line with reality, which it is hoped, might place them more noticeably before the public at large, who may then act on real school "reform."

REFERENCES

Aaron, B., Najita, J. M., & Stern, J. L. (Eds). (1988). Public Sector Bargaining (2nd ed.). Washington, D.C.: Bureau of National Affairs, Inc.

Adler, M. J. (1977). Reforming Education. New York: MacMillan.

Altenbaugh, R. J. (1989). Teachers, Their World, and Their Work: A Review of the Idea of "Professional Excellence" in School Reform Reports. In C. M. Shea, E. Kahane, & P. Sola (Eds.), The New Servants of Power: A Critique of the 1980's School Reform Movement (pp. 167-175). New York: Greenwood Press.

Alutto, J. A., & Belasco, J. A. (1976). Determinants of Attitudinal Militancy Among Teachers and Nurses. In A. M. Cresswell & M. J. Murphy (Eds.), Education and Collective Bargaining (pp. 78-94). Berkeley, CA: McCutchan Publishing Corporation.

Anderson, J. D. (1993, Winter). Power, Privilege, and Public Education: Reflections on Savage Inequalities. Educational Theory, 43(1), pp. 1-10.

Andrews, D. (1992, October). Beyond the Professionalisation of Community Work. Social Alternatives, 11(3), pp. 35-38.

Angell, G. W. (Ed.). (1981) <u>Faculty and Teacher Bargaining</u>. Lexington, MA: D.C. Heath and Company.

Apple, M. W. (1987). The De-Skilling of Teaching. In F. S. Bolin & J M. Falk (Eds.). <u>Teacher Renewal</u>. New York: Teachers College Press.

Apple, M.W. (1987). Gendered Teaching, Gendered Labor. In T. Popkewitz (Ed.), <u>Critical Studies in Teacher Education</u> (pp. 57-83). Philadelphia: The Falmer Press.

Ayers, W. (1992). Work That is Real: Why Teachers Should Be Empowered. In G. A. Hess, Jr. (Ed.), <u>Empowering Teachers and Parents</u> (pp. 13-28). Westport, CT: Bergin & Garvey.

Bacharach, S. B., Bamberger, P., Conley, S. C., Bauer, S. (1990, May). The Dimensionality of Decision Participation in Educational Organizations: The Value of a Multi-Domain Evaluative Approach, <u>Educational Administration Quarterly</u>, 26(2), pp. 126-167.

Bacharach, S. B. & B. L. Mundell (1993, November). Organizational Politics in Schools: Micro, Macro, and Logics of Action. <u>Educational Administration Quarterly</u>, 29(4), pp. 423-452.

Bakalis, M.J. (1985). <u>Report of the Illinois Project for School Reform</u>. Evanston, IL: Author.

Banks, O. (1976). <u>The Sociology of Education</u>. New York: Schocken Books.

Barringer, M.D. (1993, March). How the National Board Builds Professionalism. <u>Educational Leadership</u>, 50(6), pp. 18-22.

Barth, R. S. (1988). School: A Community of Leaders. In A. Lieberman (Ed.), <u>Building a Professional Culture in Schools</u> (pp. 129-147). New York: Teachers College Press.

Barzun, J. (1991). Begin Here: The Forgotten Conditions of Teaching and Learning. M. Philipson (Ed.). Chicago: The University of Chicago Press.

Bascia, N. (1994). Unions in Teachers' Professional Lives. New York: Teachers College Press.

Bastian, A., Fruchter, N., Gittrell, M., Greer, C., & Haskins, K. (1986). Choosing Equality: The Case for Democratic Schooling. Philadelphia: Temple University Press.

Beard, C. H. (1993, Summer). A Call to Action In a Nation Still at Risk. Journal of Staff, Program, & Organization Development, 11(2), 105-113.

Becker, H. (1962). The Nature of a Profession. In Education for the Professions. Chicago: University of Chicago Press.

Beezley, P.C. (1963). Education For What?. New York: The Bookmailer, Inc.

Bell, T. H. (1993, April). Reflections One Decade After A Nation at Risk. Phi Delta Kappan,74 (8), 592-97.

Bellah, R., Madsen, R., Sullivan, W., Swidler, A., & Tipton, S. (1985). Habits of the Heart: Individualism and Commitment in American Life. Berkeley: University of California Press.

Bellah, R., Madsen, R., Sullivan, W., Swidler, A., & Tipton, S. (1991). The Good Society. New York: Vintage Books.

Bergen, T. J., Jr. (1992, Spring). The Criticisms of Teacher Education: A Historical Perspective. Teacher Education Quarterly, 19 (2), 5-18.

Berman, E. H. (1989). The State's Stake in Educational Reform. In C. M. Shea, E. Kahane, & P. Sola (Eds.), The New Servants of Power: A Critique of the 1980's School Reform Movement (pp. 57-66). New York: Greenwood Press.

Berry, B., & Ginsberg, R. (1991). Effective Schools and Teacher Professionalism: Educational Policy at a Crossroads. In J. R. Bliss, W. A. Firestone, C. E. Richards (Eds.), Rethinking Effective Schools: Research and Practice (pp.138-153). Englewood Cliffs, NJ: Prentice Hall, Inc.

Berube, M. R. (1988). Teacher Politics. Westport, CT: Greenwood Press.

Beyer, L. E. (1992). Educational Studies, Critical Teacher Preparation and the Liberal Arts: A View From the USA. Journal of Education for Teaching, 18 (2), 131-148.

Beyer, L. E.; Feinberg, W.; Pagano, J.; Whitson, J. A. (1989). Preparing Teachers As Professionals. New York: Teachers College Record.

Blackburn, J., & Busman, G. (1977). Understanding Unions In the Public Sector, Los Angeles:Institute of Industrial Relations, UCLA.

Bledstein, B. J. (1976). The Culture of Professionalism. New York: W.W. Norton & Company, Inc.

Blum, A. A. (1993, September). Towards Industrial Democracy. Contemporary Review,263(1532), 120-126.

Blumenthal, S. (1988). Our Long National Daydream. New York: Harper & Row.

Bok, D. (1993). The Cost of Talent. New York: The Free Press.

Bolin, F. S. & Falk, J. M. (Eds.), (1987). Teacher Renewal. New York: Teachers College Press.

Booth, W.C. (1988). The Vocation of a Teacher. Chicago: The University of Chicago Press.

Boulter, W., Purvis, J., Leonard, R. (1985). Foundations of Teacher Unionism. Journal of Collective Negotiations in the Public Sector, 14(3),239-244.

Boulter, W. F. & Leonard, R. L. & Wiliams, H. S. (1989, Spring). Teacher Unionism: Factors that Motivate Membership. Journal of Collective Negotiations in the Public Sector,18,171-82.

Boyd, W. L. (1982, Summer). The Political Economy of Public Schools. Educational Adminstration Quarterly,18(3),111-130.

Boyer, E. L. (1983). High School. New York: Harper & Row.

Bracey, G. W. (1993, October). The Condition of Public Education. Phi Delta Kappan,75(2),105-117.

Brandt, R., (1993, March). Overview: What Do You Mean, 'Professional'? Educational Leadership, 50(6), 5.

Bray, R. D. (1982, Winter). Working to the Contract in Virginia: Legal Consequences of Teachers' Attempts to Limit Their Contractual Duties. University of Richmond Law Review, 16(2), 449-65.

Brint, S. (1993, August). Eliot Freidson's Contribution to the Sociology of Professions. Work and Occupations, 20(3), 259-278.

Brookover, W. B., & Erickson, E. L. (1975). Sociology of Education. Homewood, IL: The Dorsey Press.

Bull, B. L. (1990). The Limits of Teacher Professionalization. In J. I. Goodlad, R. Soder, & K. S. Sirotnik (Eds.), The Moral Dimensions of Teaching (pp. 87-129). San Francisco: Jossey-Bass Publishers.

Bull, B. L. (1993). Ethics in the Preservice Curriculum. In K. A. Strike & P. L. Ternasky (Eds.), Ethics for Professionals in Education (pp. 69-83). New York: Teachers College Press.

Bullard, P., & Taylor, B. O. (1993). Making School Reform Happen. Boston: Allyn & Bacon.

Bunzel, J. H. (Ed.). (1985). Challenge to American Schools. New York: Oxford University Press.

Burbules, N. C., & Densmore, K. (1991). The Limits of Making Teaching a Profession. Educational Policy, 5, 44-63.

Burton, J. F., & Thomason, T. (1988). The extent of Collective Bargaining in the Public Sector. In B. Aaron, J. M. Najita, & J. L. Stern (Eds.), Public Sector Bargaining (2nd ed.), (pp. 1-51). Washington, D. C.: Bureau of National Affairs, Inc.

Buss, W. G. (1979). Easy Cases Make Bad Law: Academic Expulsion and the Uncertain Law of Procedural Due Process, Iowa Law Review, 65(1), 1-101.

Butler, D. J., & Dilts, D. A. (1988). The Effectiveness of Constrained Collective Bargaining: Teacher-School Board Negotiations In Kansas, Journal of Collective Negotiations in the Public Sector, 17(1) 51-61.

Camp, W. E., & Underwood, J. K., & Connelly, M. J., & Lane, K. E. (Eds.). (1993). The Principal's Legal Handbook. Topeka, KS: National Organization on Legal Problems of Education.

Carew, J. V. & Lightfoot, S. L. (1979). Beyond Bias: Perspectives on Classrooms. Cambridge, MA:Harvard University Press.

Carnegie Forum on Education and the Economy. (1986). A Nation Prepared: Teachers for the 21st Century. New York.

Carnoy, M., and H.M. Levin. (1985). Schooling and Work in the Democratic State. Stanford, CA: Stanford University Press.

Carter, J. (1992). Turning Point. New York: Times Books.

Cheng, C. W. (1981). Teacher Unions and the Power Structure. Bloomington, IN: Phi Delta Educational Foundation.

Chomsky, N. (1991). Deterring Democracy. New York: Hill and Wang.

Chronicle of Higher Education (Ed.). (1993). Almanac of Higher Education. Chicago: University of Chicago Press.

Chubb, J. E. & Moe, T. M. (1990). Politics, Markets & America's Schools. Washington D.C.: The Brookings Institution.

Citron, C. H. (1985, July). An Overview of Legal Issues in Teacher Quality. Journal of Law and Education,14 (3),277-307.

Clark, R. T., Jr. (1981, July). Labor Relations in the Decade Ahead: A Management Perspective. Journal of Law and Education, 10 (3),365-72.

Clark, R. T., Jr. (1993, Spring). School-Based Management--Problems and Prospects. Journal of Law & Education, 22 (2), 183-86.

Clifford, G. J. & Guthrie, J. W. (1988). Ed School. Chicago: University of Chicago Press.

Clifford, P., & Friesen, S. L. (1993, Fall). A Curious Plan: Managing on the Twelfth. Harvard Educational Review, 63 (3), 339-358.

Cohen, M.L. (1978). Legal Research in a Nutshell. St. Paul, MN: West Publishing Co.

Cole, S. (1969). The Unionization of Teachers. New York: Praeger Publishers.

Coleman, J. S., Campbell, E., Hobson, C., McPartland, J., Mood, A., Weinfield, F., & York, R. (1966). Equality of Educational Opportunity. Washington D.C.: U.S. Government Printing Office.

Collins, R. (1979). The Credential Society. New York: Academic Press, Inc.

Conley, S. C. & Bacharach, S. B. (1991). From School-Site Management to Participatory School-Site Management. In S. C. Conley & B. S. Cooper (Eds.), The School as a Work Environment: Implications for Reform (pp. 127-140). Boston: Allyn & Bacon.

Conley, S. C. & Cooper, B. S. (Eds.). (1991). The School as a Work Environment: Implications for Reform. Boston: Allyn & Bacon.

Cooper, B. S. (1991). Changing Paradigms of School Organization: Implications of Teacher Collaboration on School Operations. In S. C. Conley & B. S. Cooper (Eds.), The School as a Work Environment: Implications for Reform (pp. 257-279). Boston: Allyn & Bacon.

Cooper, B. S., & Conley, S. C. (1991). From Blame to Empowerment: Critical Issues in the Teacher Work Environment. In S. C. Conley & B.S. Cooper (Eds.), The School as a Work Environment: Implications for Reform (pp. 2-16). Boston: Allyn & Bacon.

Cooper, M. (1988). Whose Culture Is It, Anyway? In A. Lieberman (Ed.), Building a Professional Culture in Schools (pp. 45-54). New York: Teachers College Press.

Cornbleth, C. (1989). Cries of Crisis, Calls for Reform, and Challenges of Change. In L. Weis, P.G. Altbach, G.P. Kelly, H.G. Petrie, & S. Slaughter (Eds.), Crisis in Teaching: Perspectives on Current Reforms (pp. 9-30). Albany, NY: State University of New York Press.

Covert, J. R. (1989, Spring). Educational Malpractice: A Threat to Administrators or Teachers. Educational Forum, 53(3),255-75.

Cresswell, A. M. & Murphy, M. J. (1976). Education and Collective Bargaining. Berkeley, CA: McCutchan Publishing Co.

Crowson, R. L. (1992). School-community Relations Under Reform. Berkeley, CA: McCutchan.

Cuban, L. (1989). The Persistence of Reform in American Schools. In D. Warren (Ed.), American Teachers: Histories of a Profession at Work (pp. 370-392). New York: Macmillan Publishing Co.

Curtin, L.L. (1994, August). Collegial Ethics of a Caring Profession. Nursing Management,25(8),pp. 28-32.

Darling-Hammond, L. (1988). Policy and Professionalism. In A. Lieberman (Ed.), Building a Professional Culture in Schools (pp. 55-77). New York: Teachers College Press.

Darling-Hammond, L., (1992, November). Reframing the School Reform Agenda. The School Administrator,49(10), 22-27.

Darling-Hammond, L. (1994, August). National Standards and Assessments: Will They Improve Education? American Journal of Education,102(4), pp. 478-510.

Davey, H.W., Bognanno, M.F., & Estenson, D.L. (1982). Contemporary Collective Bargaining (4th ed.). Englewood Cliffs, NJ: Prentice-Hall, Inc.

David, J.L. (1990). Restructuring in Progress: Lessons from pioneering districts. In R.F. Elmore and Associates, Restructuring Schools. The Next Generation of Educational Reform (pp. 209-211). San Francisco: Jossey-Bass.

Davis, G.A. & Thomas, M.A. (1989). Effective Schools and Effective Teachers. Boston: Allyn and Bacon.

Densmore, K. (1987). Professionalism, Proletarianization and Teacher Work. In T. Popkewitz (Ed.), Critical Studies in Teacher Education (pp. 130-160). Philadelphia: The Falmer Press.

Devaney, K. & Sykes, G. (1988). Making the Case for Professionalism. In A. Lieberman (Ed.), Building a Professional Culture in Schools (pp. 3-22). New York: Teachers College Press.

Developments in the Law - Public Employment. (1984, May). Harvard Law Review,97(7),1611-1800.

DeYoung, A.J. (1986, Spring). Excellence in Education: The Opportunity for School Superintendents to Become Ambitious? Educational Administration Quarterly,22(2),91-113.

Dilts, D.A. (1986). The Negotiation of Teacher Economic Packages: An Analysis of Kansas' Settlements for 1983 and 1984. Journal of Collective Negotiations in the Public Sector,15(3),273-280.

Dilts, D.A., Boyda, S.W., Sherr, M.A., (1993). Collective Bargaining in the Absence of Protective Legislation: The Case of Louisiana. Journal of Collective Negotiations in the Public Sector,22 (3),259-65.

Dilts, D.A., & Walsh, W.J. (1988). Collective Bargaining and Impasse Resolution in the Public Sector. New York: Quorum Press.

Dingwall, R., & Lewis, P. (Eds.).(1983). The Sociology of the Professions. London: Macmillan Press Ltd.

Dobay, C. V. (1988). Seeds of Mediocrity. Lanham, MD: University Press of America, Inc.

Doherty, R. E. (1979). On the Merits of Greater Public Access to the Bargaining Process: An Equivocal View. In R.E. Doherty (Ed.),Public Access: Citizens and Collective Bargaining in the Schools (pp. 1-7). Ithaca, NY: Cornell University Press.

Dunklee, D. R., & Shoop, R. J. (1993). A Primer for School Risk Management. Boston: Allyn & Bacon.

Dunklin, M., & Biddle, B. (1974). The Study of Teaching. NY: Holt.

Dupont, R. P., & Tobin, R. D. (1971, Summer). Teacher Negotiations into the Seventies. William & Mary Law Review, 12 (4),711-49.

Dzuback, M. A. (1993, Fall). Professionalism, Higher Education, and American Culture: Burton J. Bledstein's The Culture of Professionalism. History of Education Quarterly 33(3),375-385.

Eberts, R.W. & Stone, J.A. (1984). Unions and Public Schools. Lexington, MA: D.C. Heath and Co.

Edwards, R. (1993). Rights at Work. Washington, D.C.: The Brookings Institution.

Eisner, E.W. (1992, Summer). Educational Reform and the Ecology of Schooling. Teachers College Record, 93 (4),610-627.

Elam, S. (1979, January). Some Overactions on Competence, Phi Delta Kappan,60(5),337.

Elam, S. M.; Rose, L. C.; Gallup, A. M. (1993, October). The 25th Annual Phi Delta Kappa Gallup Poll of the Public's Attitudes Toward the Public Schools. Phi Delta Kappan,75(2),137-152.

Elkin, S. M. (1979). Another Look at Collective Negotiations for Professionals. In M. J. Levine & E. C. Hagburg, Labor Relations in the Public Sector (pp. 85-94). Salt Lake City, UT: Brighton Publishing Co.

Elmore, R. F. (1990). On Changing the Structure of Public Schools. In R. F. Elmore and Associates, Restructuring Schools (pp. 1-28). San Francisco: Jossey-Bass Publishers.

Etzioni,A. (1969). The Semi-Professions and Their Organization. New York: Free Press.

Etzioni, A. (1988). The Moral Dimension Toward a New Economics. New York: Free Press.

Fantini, M. D. (1974). What's Best for the Children. Garden City, New York: Anchor Press.

Farrar, E. (1990). Reflections on the First Wave of Reform: Reordering America's Educational Priorities. In S. L. Jacobsen & J. A. Conway (Eds.), Educational Leadership in an Age of Reform (pp. 3-13). NY: Longman Press.

Feinberg, W. (1990). The Moral Responsibility of Public Schools. In J. I. Goodlad, (Ed.), The Moral Dimensions of Teaching (pp. 155-187). San Francisco: Jossey-Bass Publishers.

Feinberg, W., & Soltis, J. F. (1985). School and Society. NY: Teachers College Press.

Felker, L. S., Griffith, E. R., Durrant, E. W. (1984). Public Sector Unionization in the South: An Agenda for Research. Journal of Collective Negotiations in the Public Sector, 13(1), 1-13

Fenstermacher, G.D. (1990). Some Moral Considerations on Teaching as a Profession. In J.I. Goodlad, R. Soder, & K.S. Sirotnik (Eds.), The Moral Dimensions of Teaching (pp. 130-154). San Francisco: Jossey-Bass Publishers.

Feuille, P., (1991, Fall). Unionism in the Public Sector: The Joy of Protected Markets. Journal of Labor Research,12,351-67.

Fick, B. J. (1989, Fall). Negotiation Theory and the Law of Collective Bargaining. Kansas Law Review,38,81-99.

Finch, M., & Nagel, T. W. (1983). Collective Bargaining in the Public Schools: Reassessing Labor Policy in an Era of Reform. Wisconsin Law Review,6,1573-1670.

Finn, C.E. (1985). Teacher Unions and School Quality: Potential Allies or Inevitable Foes. In J.H. Bunzel (Ed.), Challenge to American Schools (pp. 99-126). New York: Oxford University Press.

Finn, C. E. (1991). We Must Take Charge. New York: The Free Press.

Finn, C. E. & Rebarber, T. (Eds.). (1992). Education Reform in the 90's. New York: Macmillan Publishing.

Firestone, W. A. (1993, March). Why 'Professionalizing' Teaching Is Not Enough. Educational Leadership, 50 (6),6-11.

Firestone, W. A. & Bader, B. D. (1992). Redesigning Teaching: Professionalism or Bureaucracy. Albany, NY: State University of New York Press.

First, P. F. (1992). Educational Policy for School Administrators. Boston: Allyn & Bacon.

Fischer, L., Schimmel, D., & Kelly, C. (1991). Teachers and the Law. White Plains, NY: Longman Publishing Group.

Fox, M.J., & Amon, I.W. (1993). The Reshaping of Nonrenewal and Termination Practices Regarding Teacher Contracts: A Texas Focus. Journal of Collective Negotiations, 22 (1),13-29.

Fox, M. (1993). Radical Reflections:Passionate Opinions on Teaching, Learning, and Living. San Diego:Harcourt Brace & Company.

Fraser, J. W. (1989). Agents of Democracy: Urban Elementary School Teachers and the Conditions of Teaching. In D. Warren (Ed.), American Teachers (pp. 118-156). New York: Macmillan Publishing Co.

Freidson, E. (Ed.). (1971). The Professions and Their Prospects. Beverly Hills, CA: Sage Publications, Inc.

Freidson, E. (1986). Professional Powers. Chicago: University of Chicago Press.

Fullan, M.G. (with S.M. Stiegelbauer). (1991). The New Meaning of Educational Change (2nd. ed.). Englewood Cliffs, NJ: Prentice-Hall.

Fullan, M.G. (1993, March). Why Teachers Must Become Change Agents. Educational Leadership,50 (6), 12-17.

Futrell, M.H. (1993, Summer). K-12 Education Reform: A View From the Trenches. Educational Record, 74 (3), 6-14.

Gage, N.L. (1978). The Scientific Basis of the Art of Teaching. New York: Teachers College Press.

Gage, N. L. (1985). Hard Gains in the Soft Sciences. Bloomington, IN: Phi Delta Kappa.

Gardner, H. (1991). The Unschooled Mind. New York: Basic Books.

Gatto, J. T. (1993). The Exhausted School: The First National Speakout on the Right to School Choice. New York: The Odysseus Group.

Gee, E. G. (1979, Summer). The Unionization of Mr. Chips: A Survey of Collective Bargaining in the Public Schools. Willamette Law Review, 15(3),367-460.

Geiger, K. (1992, Summer). America 2000: New Direction or Misdirection? Kansas Journal of Law & Public Policy, 2 (2), 85-96.

Gely, R., & Chandler, T. D. (1993, Fall). Determinants of Management's Organizational Structure in the Public Sector. Journal of Labor Research,14(4), 381-97.

Genck, F. H. (1991). Renewing America's Progress. New York: Praeger Publishers.

Gerhart, P. F. (April 1976). Determinants of Bargaining Outcomes in Local Government Labor Negotiations. Industrial and Labor Relations Review, 29(3),331-351.

Gideonse, H.D. (1993, December). The Governance of Teacher Education and Systemic Reform. Educational Policy,7(4), 395-426.

Ginsburg, M. (1987). Reproduction, Contradiction and Conceptions of Professionalism: The Case of Pre-Service Teachers. In T. Popkewitz (Ed.), Critical Studies in Teacher Education (pp. 86-129). Philadelphia: The Falmer Press.

Giroux, H. A. (1988). Teachers As Intellectuals. Granby, MA: Bergin & Garvey Publishers, Inc.

Glatthorn, A. A. (1992). Teachers as Agents of Change: A New Look at School Improvement. Washington, D.C.: National Education Association.

Glazer, N. (1988). The Limits of Social Policy. Cambridge, MA: Harvard University Press.

Goens, G.A. & Clover, S.I.R. (1991). Mastering School Reform. Boston: Allyn and Bacon.

Goetz, R., (1980, Winter). The Kansas Public Employer-Employee Relations Law. Kansas Law Review, 28, 243-89.

Goldberg, M. F. (1993, March). A Portrait of Albert Shanker. Educational Leadership, 50(6), 46-49.

Goldschmidt, S.M. & Painter, S.R. (1987-88) Collective Bargaining: A Review of the Literature. Educational Research Quarterly, 12(1), 10-24.

Gonder, P.O. (1981). Collective Bargaining, AASA Critical Issues Report, Sacramento: AASA.

Goodlad, J., & Oakes, J. (1988). We Must Offer Equal Access to Knowledge. Educational Leadership,45, 16-22.

Goodlad, J.I. (1990). Teachers For Our Nation's Schools. San Francisco: Jossey-Bass Publishers.

Goodlad, J.I.; Soder, R., Sirotnik, K.A. (Eds.). (1990). The Moral Dimensions of Teaching. San Francisco: Jossey-Bass Publishers.

Goodwin, A.L. (1987). Vocational Choice and the Realities of Teaching. In F.S. Bolin & J.M. Falk, (Eds.), Teacher Renewal (pp. 30-36). New York: Teachers College Press.

Goodwin, R.N. (1992). Promises to Keep. New York: Times Books.

Gould, W.B., IV (1986). A Primer on American Labor Law, (2nd ed.). Cambridge, MA: The MIT Press.

Graham, P.A. (1992). S. O. S. Sustain Our Schools. New York: Hill and Wang.

Grant, G. (1993). Discovering How You Really Teach. In K.A. Strike & P. L. Ternasky (Eds.), Ethics for Professionals in Education (pp. 135-147). New York: Teachers College Press.

Grodin, J.R.; Wollett, D.H.; Alleyne, R.H., Jr. (1979). Collective Bargaining in Public Employment. Washington, D.C.: The Bureau of National Affairs, Inc.

Gross, J. A. (1988). Teachers on Trial. Ithaca, NY: Cornell University Press.

Gutmann, A. (1987). Democratic Education. Princeton, NJ: Princeton University Press.

Haberman, M. (1986). Licensing Teachers: Lessons from other professions. Phi Delta Kappan,67(10), 719-722.

Haley, J.F. (1946, November). Teaching-A Profession. Educational Forum, 11(1), reprinted (1993, Winter), Educational Forum,57(2), 204-208.

Hammond, G.L. (1980). Contract terminations of Iowa public school teachers: considerations of the substantive content of "just cause" for termination. Drake Law Review,30(1),123-144.

Hansen, D.T. (1994, Summer). Teaching and the Sense of Vocation. Educational Theory,44(3),pp. 259-275.

Hansen, R.L., Allen, J.B. (1985, July). Public Referendum: Is it an Effective Mechanism for Resolving Collective Bargaining Impasses? A Union Perspective. Journal of Law and Education,14(3),471-482.

Hanson, E.M. (1991). Educational Restructuring in the USA: Movements of the 1980's. Journal of Educational Administration, 29(4),30-38.

Havighurst, R.J., & Neugarten, B.L. (1975). Society and Education, 4th ed., Boston: Allyn and Bacon, Inc.

Hawkins, R.B., Jr. (1985). A Strategy for Revitalizing Public Education. In J.H. Bunzel (Ed.), Challenge to American Schools (pp. 29-46). New York: Oxford University Press.

Herbst, J. (1989). And Sadly Teach: Teacher Education and Professionalization in American Culture. Madison: University of Wisconsin Press.

Herbst, J. (1989). Teacher Preparation in the Nineteenth Century: Institutions and Purposes. In D. Warren (Ed.), American Teachers (pp. 213-236). New York: Macmillan Publishing Co.

Herndon, T. (1983). We, the Teachers. Cabin John, MD: Seven Locks Press.

Hess, G.A.,Jr. (Ed.). (1992). Empowering Teachers and Parents. Westport, CT: Bergin & Garvey.

Hogan, J.C. (1985). The Schools, the Courts, and the Public Interest. Lexington, MA: Lexington Press.

Hogler, R.L., Thompson, M.J. (1985, July). Collective Negotiations in Education and the Public Interest: A Proposed Method of Impasse Resolution. Journal of Law and Education,14(3),443-469.

Holdaway,E.A.,Johnson,N.A.,Ratsoy,E.W.,Friesen,D.,(1994,Summer). The Value of an Internship Program for Beginning Teachers. Educational Evaluation and Policy Analysis,16(2),pp. 205-221.

Holmes, M., & Wynne, E.A. (1989). Making the School an Effective Community. New York: The Falmer Press.

Hoover, K.R. (1980). The Elements of Social Scientific Thinking, (2nd ed.). New York: St. Martin's Press.

Hostetler, K., (1989, May). Who Says Professional Ethics is Dead? A Response to Myron Lieberman. Phi Delta Kappan,70(9), 723-25.

Howe, K. R. (1993). The Liberal Democratic Tradition and Educational Ethics. In K.A. Strike & P.L. Ternasky (Eds.), Ethics for Professionals in Education (pp. 27-42). New York: Teachers College Press.

Hudgins, H.C., Jr. (1992). Courts as Educational Policy Makers: An Historical Perspective. In P.F. First, Educational Policy for School Administrators (pp. 79-86). Boston: Allyn & Bacon.

Hughes, E. C., Thorne, B., DeBaggis, A. M., Gurin, A., Williams, D. (1973). Education for the Professions of Medicine, Law, Theology, and Social Welfare, New York: McGraw Hill.

Imber, M. & Neidt, W.A. (1990). Teacher Participation in School Decision Making. In P. Reyes (ed.), Teachers and Their Workplace (pp. 67-85). Newbury Park, CA: Sage Publications, Inc.

Jackson, P. W. (1990). The Future of Teaching. In F.S. Bolin & J.M. Falk (Eds.), Teacher Renewal (pp. 43-58). New York: Teachers College Press.

Jacobsen, G.S., Sperry, D., Jensen, B. (1972, July). The Dismissal and Non-Reemployment of Teachers. Journal of Law and Education, 1(3), 435-448.

Jacobstein, J.M. & Mersky, R.M. (1977). Fundamentals of Legal Research. Mineola, NY: The Foundation Press, Inc.

Jarolimek, J. (1981). The Schools in Contemporary Society. New York: Macmillan Publishing Co., Inc.

Jencks, C. (1972). Inequality: A Reassessment of the effect of family and schooling in America. New York: Harper & Row.

Jerry, R.H., II, (1981, Winter). Recovery in Tort for Educational Malpractice: Problems of Theory and Policy. Kansas Law Review, 29, 195-212.

Jessup, D.K. (1978, January). Teacher Unionization: A Reassessment of Rank and File Motivations. Sociology of Education,51,44-55.

Johnson, S.M. (1984). Teacher Unions in Schools. Philadelphia: Temple University Press.

Johnson, S.M. (1990). Redesigning Teachers' Work. In R.F. Elmore and Associates, Restructuring Schools (pp. 125-151). San Francisco: Jossey-Bass Publishers.

Jones, B.L. & Maloy, R.W. (1988). Partnerships for Improving Schools. New York: Greenwood Press.

Judge, H. (1988). Afterword. In A. Lieberman (Ed.), Building a Professional Culture in Schools (pp. 222-231). New York: Teachers College Press.

Kantrowitz, B., Wingert, P., Chideya, F., Springen, K., Rosenberg, D., & King, P. (1993, April 19). A Nation Still At Risk. Newsweek, pp. 46-49.

Katz, M.B. (1992, Fall). Chicago School Reform as History. Teachers College Record,94(1), 56-72.

Katznelson, I., & Weir, M. (1985). Schooling For All. New York: Basic Books, Inc.

150   *The Professionalization of Teaching*

Kay, W.F. (1973, January). The Need for Limitation Upon the Scope 6 Negotiations In Public Education, II. <u>Journal of Law and Education</u>,2(1),155-75.

Kearney, R.C. (1984). <u>Labor Relations in the Public Sector</u>. New York:Marcel Dekker, Inc.

Keast, W.R., & Commission on Academic Tenure in Higher Education (Eds.). (1973). <u>Faculty Tenure</u>. San Francisco: Jossey-Bass.

Keith, S., & Girling, R.H. (1991). <u>Education, Management, and Participation</u>. Boston: Allyn and Bacon.

Kerchner, C.T. (1993, November). Building the Airplane as it Rolls Down the Runway:Administrators Discover Labor Relations as the Linchpin to School Change. <u>School Administrator</u>,10(50),8-15.

Kerchner, C.T. & Caufman, K.D. (1993). Building the Airplane While It's Rolling Down the Runway. In C.T. Kerchner & J.E. Koppich (Eds.), <u>A Union of Professionals</u> (pp. 1-24). New York: Teachers College Press.

Kerchner, C.T. & Koppich, J.E. (1991). Redefining Teacher Work Roles through the Educational Policy Trust Agreement. In S.C. Conley & B.S. Cooper (Eds.), <u>The School as a Work Environment: Implications for Reform</u> (pp. 237-255). Boston: Allyn & Bacon.

Kerchner, C.T., & Mitchell,D. (1988). <u>The Changing Idea of a Teachers' Union</u>. NY: Falmer Press.

Kidder, T. (1989). <u>Among Schoolchildren</u>. Boston: Houghton Mifflin Company.

Kimball, B.A. (1988, Winter). The Problem of Teacher's Authority in Light of the Structural Analysis of Professions. <u>Educational Theory</u>,38(8),1-9.

Kimbrough, R.B. (1982, Spring). Do Political Ideologies Influence Education in the United States? Educational Administration Quarterly,18(2),22-38.

Kohl, P.L. (1992, Fall). Sharing the Power: Fact or Fallacy? Action in Teacher Education, 14(3), 29-36.

Koppich, J.E. (1993). Getting Started: A Primer on Professional Unionism. In C.T. Kerchner & J.E. Koppich (Eds.), A Union of Professionals (pp. 194-204). New York: Teachers College Press.

Kottkamp, R.B. (1990). Teacher Attitudes About Work. In P. Reyes (ed.), Teachers and Their Workplace (pp. 86-114). Newbury Park, CA: Sage Publications, Inc.

Kozak, F.R. (1977, Winter). Public Employee Collective Bargaining in Virginia: Perspectives and Direction. University of Richmond Law Review,11(2),431-45.

Kraybill, D. & Pellman Good, P. (Eds.), (1982). Perils of Professionalism. Scottdale: Herald Press.

Kuenzbi, A. (1945, September). Dismissal or Removal of Public School Teachers Under Teacher's Tenure Laws. Notre Dame Lawyer,21,25-39.

Kultgen, J. (1988). Ethics and Professionalism. Philadelphia: University of Pennsylvania Press.

Kurth, M. (1987, Fall). Teachers' Unions and Excellence in Education: An Analysis of the Decline in SAT Scores. Journal of Labor Research, 8,351-67.

Kurth, M. (1988, Fall). Teachers' Unions and Excellence in Education: Reply. Journal of Labor Research,9,389-94.

Labaree, D.F. (1992, Summer). Power, Knowledge, and the Rationalization of Teaching: A Genealogy of the Movement to Professionalize n Teachig. <u>Harvard Educational Review</u>,62(2),123-154.

LaMorte, M.W. (1992). <u>School Law</u> (4th ed.). Englewood Cliffs, NJ: Prentice-Hall, Inc.

Larson, M. (1977). <u>The Rise of Professionalism - A Sociological Analysis</u>. Berkeley, CA: University of California Press.

Latham, G. (1993, February). Do Educators Use the Literature of the Profession? <u>NASSP Bulletin</u>,77(550), 63-70.

Lawn, M., & Grace, G. (Eds.). (1987). <u>Teachers: The Culture and Politics of Work</u>. Philadelphia: The Falmer Press.

Leap, T. L. (1991). <u>Collective Bargaining and Labor Relations</u>. New York: MacMillan Publishing Co.

Leibig, M.T. & Kahn, W.L. (1987). <u>Public Employee Organizing and the Law</u>. Washington, D.C.: The Bureau of National Affairs, Inc.

Levine, M.J., & Hagburg, E.C. (1979). <u>Labor Relations in the Public Sector</u>. Salt Lake City, UT: Brighton Publishing Company.

Levine, M.J., & Hagburg, E.C. (1979). <u>Public Sector Labor Relations</u>. St. Paul, MN: West Publishing Co.

Lewis, A.C. (1993, April). The Teaching 'Profession' Goes National. <u>Phi Delta Kappan</u>,74(8), 588-89.

Lewis, J., Jr. (1971). <u>The Tragedies in American Education</u>. New York: Exposition Press.

Lieberman, A. (Ed.). (1988). <u>Building a Professional Culture in Schools</u>. New York:Teachers College Press.

Lieberman, A., Saxl, E.R., Miles, M.B.(1988). Teacher Leadership: Ideology and Practice. In A. Lieberman (Ed.), Building a Professional Culture in Schools (pp. 148-166). New York: Teachers College Press.

Lieberman, A. & Miller, L. (1978, September). The Social Realities of Teaching. Teachers College Record,80(1),54-68.

Lieberman, M., (1988, October). Professional Ethics in Public Education: An Autopsy. Phi Delta Kappan,70(2),159-60.

Lieberman, M.,(1989, Winter). Alternatives to Teacher Unions. Government Union Review,10,14-26.

Lifton, F.B. (1992, January). The Legal Tangle of Shared Governance. The School Administrator,49(1),16-19.

Lightfoot, S.L. (1979). The Teacher as Central Figure. In J.V. Carew and Sara L. Lightfoot, Beyond Bias: Perspectives on Classrooms (pp. 5-24). Cambridge, MA: Harvard University Press.

Lightfoot, S.L. (1979). The Social Context of School and Community. In J.V. Carew and S.L. Lightfoot, Beyond Bias: Perspectives on Classrooms (pp. 53-68). Cambridge, MA: Harvard University Press.

Lightfoot, S.L. (1987). On Excellence and Goodness. Harvard Educational Review,57,202-205.

Livingston, C. (1992). Teachers as Leaders: Evolving Roles. Washington, D.C.: National Education Association.

Lortie, D.C. (1975). Schoolteacher. Chicago: University of Chicago Press.

Loscalzo, T.E. (1985, October). Liability for Malpractice in Education. Journal of Law and Education,14(4), 595-607.

Lowe, R. (1993, Winter). Constricted Terrain: Jonathan Kozol, The Left, and the Possibilities of Educational Reform. Educational Theory,43(1),11-14.

Lynn, K.S. (Ed.). (1963). The Professions in America. Boston: Beacon Press.

Maccoby, M. (1992, March/April). The New Unionism. Utne Reader,50, 85-87.

Macmillan, C.J.B. (1993). Ethics and Teacher Professionalization. In K. A. Strike & P.L. Ternasky (Eds.), Ethics for Professionals in Education (pp. 189-201). New York: Teachers College Press.

Maddaus, J. (1992). The Politics of Parental Choice. In Patricia F. First, Educational Policy for School Administrators (pp. 29-37). Boston: Allyn & Bacon.

Maeroff, G.I. (1988). The Empowerment of Teachers. New York: Teachers College Press.

Maguire, J.W. (1979). Professional Negotiations: State or Federal Legislation? In Levine and Hagburg, Labor Relations in the Public Sector (pp. 91-94). Salt Lake City, UT: Brighton Publishing Co.

Marett, P.C., & Jedel, M.J. (1988). Public Sector Labor Relations in the Southeast: A Five-State Update. Journal of Collective Negotiations in the Public Sector,17(2),145-152.

Martin, D.T. (1989). A Critique of the Concept of Work and Education in the School Reform Reports. In C.M. Shea, E. Kahane, & P. Sola (Eds.), The New Servants of Power: A Critique of the 1980's School Reform Movement (pp. 39-56). New York: Greenwood Press.

Mattingly, P.H. (1987). Workplace Autonomy and the Reforming of Teacher Education. In T.Popkewitz (Ed.), Critical Studies in Teacher Education (pp.36-56). Philadelphia: The Falmer Press.

Mayhew, L.B. (1971). Changing Practices in Education for the Professions. Atlanta: Southern Regional Education Board.

McCarthy, M.M. & Cambron-McCabe, N.H. (1987). Public School Law. Newton, MA: Allyn & Bacon.

McDonnell,L. (1991). Ideas and values in implementation analysis: The case of teacher policy. In A.R. Odden (Ed.), Education Policy Implementation (pp. 241-258). Albany: State University of New York Press.

McDonnell, L., & Pascal, A.,(1979). Organized Teachers in American Schools. R-2407-NIE. Rand Corporation, Santa Monica, CA

McNeil, L.M. (1989). Exit, Voice, and Community: Magnet Teachers' Responses to Standardization. In L. Weis, P.G. Altbach, G.P. Kelly, H. G. Petrie, & S. Slaughter (Eds.), Crisis in Teaching: Perspectives on Current Reforms (pp. 159-181). Albany: State University of New York Press.

McLaughlin, M.W., & Talbert, J.E. (1993). Contexts That Matter For Teaching and Learning: Strategic Opportunities for Meeting the Nation's Educational Goals. Stanford, CA: Center for Research on the Context of Secondary School Teaching.

Meier, D. (1992, Summer). Reinventing Teaching. Teachers College Record, 93(4), 594-609.

Meier, D. (1995). The Power of Their Ideas: Lessons for America from a Small School in Harlem. Boston: Beacon Press.

Metzler, J.H. (1973, January). The Need for Limitation Upon the Scope of Negotiations in Public Education, I. Journal of Law and Education, 2(1),139-54.

Mitchell, D. (1989). Measuring up: Standards for evaluating school reform. In T.J. Sergiovanni and J.H. Moore (Eds.), Schooling for Tomorrow: Directing Reforms to Issues that count (pp. 42-60). Needham Heights, MA: Allyn & Bacon.

Moll, R. W. (1990). The Lure of the Law. New York, NY: Viking.

Morris, A.A. (1989). The Constitution and American Public Education. Durham, NC: Carolina Academic Press.

Murphy, J. (1991). Restructuring Schools. New York: Teachers College Press.

Murphy, J., (1993, April). What's In? What's Out? American Education in the Nineties. Phi Delta Kappan,74(8),641-46.

Murphy, M. (1990). Blackboard Unions. Ithaca, NY: Cornell University Press.

Murphy, M.J., & Hoover, D. (1976). Negotiations at the Crossroads: Increased Professionalization or Reinforced Bureaucracy. In A.M. Cresswell & M.J. Murphy, (Eds.), Education and Collective Bargaining (pp. 476-483). Berkeley, CA: McCutchan Publishing Corporation.

Murray, C.E. (1992, Winter). Teaching as a Profession: The Rochester Case in Historical Perspective. Harvard Educational Review,62(4), 494-518.

National Commission on Excellence in Education. (1983). A Nation at Risk: The Imperative for Educational Reform. Washington, D.C.: U.S. Government Printing Office.

National Education Association Handbook 1992-1993, Washington, D.C. National Education Association.

Nelson, F.H., & Gould, J.C. (1988, Fall). Teachers' Unions and Excellence in Education: Comment. Journal of Labor Research,9,379-87.

Nelson, J.L., & Besag, F.P. (1970). Sociological Perspectives in Education. New York: Pitman Publishing Corporation.

Nesbitt, M.B. (1976). Labor Relations in the Federal Government

Service. In J. Grodin, D.H. Wollett, R.H. Alleyne, Jr. (Eds.), Collective Bargaining in Public Employment (pp. 11-17). Washington, D.C.: The Bureau of National Affairs, Inc.

Noblit, G.W. & Pink, W.T. (Eds.). (1987). Schooling in Social Context. Norwood,NJ: Ablex Publishing Corporation.

Noddings, N. (1993, Winter). For All Its Children. Educational Theory, 43(1),15-22.

Nyberg, D.A. (1990). Power, Empowerment, and Educational Authority. In S.L. Jacobson & J.A. Conway (Eds.), Educational Leadership in an age of Reform (pp. 47-64). NY: Longman Press.

Nystrand, R.O. (1992, November). The New Agenda for the Nation's Schools. Education and Urban Society,25(1),18-29.

Odden, A.R. (1992). School Finance and Education Reform: An Overview. In A.R. Odden (Ed.), Rethinking School Finance (pp. 1-40). San Francisco: Jossey-Bass Publishers.

Olson, M. (1965). The Logic of Collective Action. Cambridge, MA: Harvard University Press.

O'Reilly, R.C. & Green, E.T. School Law For the 1990's. New York: Greenwood Press.

Ornstein, A. (Winter, 1995). The New Paradigm in Research on Teaching. The Educational Forum,59(2), pp. 124-129.

Osterman, M.H., Jr., (1985). Collective Negotiations in Public Education. In The Evolving Process-Collective Negotiations in Public Employment, Association of Labor Relations Agencies (Ed.), Fort Washington, PA: Labor Relations Press.

Ostrander, K.H. (1987). The Legal Structure of Collective Bargaining in Education. New York:Greenwood Press.

Partridge, D.M. (1992). A Cross-Sectional Analysis of Teacher Strike Activity. <u>Journal of Collective Negotiations in the Public Sector,</u> <u>21</u>(1),27-43.

Passow, A. (1984, April). Tackling the Reform Reports of the 1980's. <u>Phi Delta Kappan,65,</u>674-683.

Paulsen, R. (1991, April). Education, Social Class, and Participation in Collective Action. <u>Sociology of Education,64</u>(2),96-110.

Perry, Charles R.,and Wildman, Wesley A. (1970). <u>The Impact of Negotiations in Public Education.</u> Belmont, CA: Wadsworth Publishing Co.,Inc.

Petrie, H.G. (1990). Reflections on the Second Wave of Reform: Restructuring the Teaching Profession. In S.L. Jacobson & J.A. Conway (Eds.), <u>Educational Leadership in an age of Reform</u>
(pp. 14- 29). NY: Longman Press.

Pink, W.T. (1989). The New Equity: Competing Visions. In C.M. Shea, E. Kahane, & P. Sola (Eds.), <u>The New Servants of Power: A Critique of the 1980's School Reform Movement</u> (pp. 123-134). New York: Greenwood Press.

Pisapia, J.R. (1981, January). The Open Bargaining Model. <u>Journal of Law and Education,10</u>(1),65-76.

Piskulich, J.P. (1992). <u>Collective Bargaining in State and Local Government.</u> New York: Praeger Publishers.

Poltrock, L.A. (1981, July). Labor Relations in the Decade Ahead: A Union Perspective. <u>Journal of Law and Education,10</u>(3),373-80.

Poltrock, L.A. (1984, July). Educational Reform and Its Labor Relations Impact From A Union Perspective. <u>Journal of Law and Education,</u> <u>13</u>(3),457-475.

Poltrock, L.A., & Goss, S.M.(1993, Spring). A Union Lawyer's View of Restructuring and Reform. Journal of Law & Education,22(2),177-82.

Popkewitz, T.S. (1985, April). What is Curriculum: The project and its prospects, paper prepared for the annual meeting of the American Educational Research Association, Chicago. In T.S. Popkewitz (Ed.), Critical Studies in Teacher Education (pp.335-354). Philadelphia: The Falmer Press.

Popkewitz, T.S. (Ed.). (1987). Critical Studies in Teacher Education. Philadelphia: The Falmer Press.

Popkewitz, T.S. (1987). Ideology and Social Formation in Teacher Education. In T. Popkewitz (Ed.), Critical Studies in Teacher Education (pp. 2-33). Philadelphia: The Falmer Press.

Postman, N. & Weingartner, C. (1969). Teaching as a Subversive Activity. New York: Delacorte Press.

Presseisen, B.Z. (1985). Unlearned Lessons. Philadelphia: Falmer Press.

Prestine, N.A. & Bowen, C. (1993, Fall). Benchmarks of Change: Assessing Essential School Restructuring Efforts. Educational Evaluation and Policy Analysis,15(3),298-319.

Purkey, S.C., & Smith, M.S. (1982). Too soon to cheer? Synthesis of research on effective schools. Educational Leadership,40(3),64-69.

Purkey, S.C., & Smith, M.S. (1985). School Reform: The district policy implications of the effective schools literature. Elementary School Journal,85,353-389.

Rabban, D.M. (1991, October). Is Unionization Compatible with Professionalism? Industrial and Labor Relations Review,45(1),97-112.

Rauth, M. (1990, June). Exploring Heresy in Collective Bargaining and School Restructuring. Phi Delta Kappan,71,781-790.

Ravitch, D. (1983). The Troubled Crusade: American Education 1945-1980. NY: Basic Books.

Raywid, M.A. (1990). Rethinking School Governance. In R.E. Elmore and Associates, Restructuring Schools (pp. 152-205). San Francisco: Jossey-Bass Publishers.

Reagan, T. (1989). More of the Same: Reforms of American Public Schooling and the Minority Language Student. In C.M. Shea, E. Kahane, & P. Sola (Eds.), The New Servants of Power: A Critique of the 1980's School Reform Movement (pp. 103-112). New York: Greenwood Press.

Rebore, R.W. (1984). A Handbook For School Board Members. Englewood Cliffs, NJ: Prentice-Hall, Inc.

Register, C.A., & Grimes, P.W. (1991, Spring). Collective Bargaining, Teachers, and Student Achievement. Journal of Labor Research,12(2),99-109.

Reglin, G.L. (1992). Public School Educators' Knowledge of Selected Supreme Court Decisions Affecting Daily Public School Operations. Journal of Educational Administration,30(2),26-31.

Reich, R.B. (1989). The Resurgent Liberal. New York: Times Books.

Reid, J.D.,Jr. & Kurth, M.M. (1990, Winter). Union Militancy Among Public Employees: A Public Choice Hypothesis. Journal of Labor Research,11(1),1-23.

Reutter,E.,Jr. (1988). The Law of Public Education (3rd. ed.). Mineola, NY:Foundation Press.

Reyes,P. (Ed.). (1990). Teachers and their Workplace. Newbury Park, CA: Sage Publications, Inc.

Rhodes, T.L., & Brown, R.G. (1992). Divided We Fall: Employee Perceptions of a Legal Prohibition on Collective Bargaining: A Preliminary Look. Journal of Collective Negotiations in the Public Sector,21(1),1-14.

Richards, R.R., Carlton, P.W. (1983). Relative Deprivation and Teacher Militancy in Virginia: A Model and its Application. Journal of Collective Negotiations in the Public Sector,12(4),355-361.

Roeder, P.W. & Whitaker, G. (1993, February). Education for the Public Service. Administration & Society,24(4),512-540.

Rosenberger, D.S., & Plimpton, R.A. (1975, July). Teacher Incompetence and the Courts. Journal of Law and Education,4(3),469-86.

Rossow, L.F. & Parkinson, J. (1992). The Law of Teacher Evaluation. Topeka, KS: National Organization on Legal Problems of Education.

Roth, R.A. (1992, Spring). Dichotomous Paradigms For Teacher Education: The Rise or Fall of the Empire. Action in Teacher Education,14(1), 1-9.

Rothman, E.P. (1977). Troubled Teachers. New York: David McKay Company, Inc.

Rowan, B. (1990). Applying Conceptions of Teaching to Organizational Reform. In R.F. Elmore and Associates, Restructuring Schools (pp. 31-58). San Francisco: Jossey-Bass Publishers.

Rowan, B. (1994, August-September). Comparing Teachers' Work with Work in Other Occupations: Notes on the Professional Status of Teaching. Educational Researcher,23(6),pp. 4-17,21.

Rury, J. L. (1989). Who Became Teachers? In D. Warren (Ed.), American Teachers (pp. 9-48). New York: Macmillan Publishing Co.

Rutter, M., Maughan, B., Mortimore, P., Ouston, J., & Smith, A. (1979). Fifteen Thousand Hours: Secondary Schools and Their Effect on Children. Cambridge, MA: Harvard University Press.

Rynecki, S.B., & Lindquist, J.H. (1988, Summer). Teacher Evaluation and Collective Bargaining A Management Perspective. Journal of Law and Education,17(3),487-506.

Rynecki, S.B., & Pickering, W.C. (1984, July). Educational Reform and Its Labor Relations From A Management Perspective. Journal of Law and Education,13(3),477-507.

Salser, C.W. & West, F. (1991). The Decline and Fall of American Education. Portland, OR:Halcyon House.

Sanders, T. (1993, October). A State Superintendent Looks at National Accreditation. Phi Delta Kappan,75(2),165-170.

Schein, E.H. (1972). Professional Education. New York: McGraw-Hill.

Seeley, D.S. (1979). The Basis for a New Parent-Teacher Relationship in Collective Bargaining. In R.E. Doherty (Ed.), Public Access: Citizens and Collective Bargaining in the Schools (pp. 29-30). Ithaca, NY: Cornell University Press.

Segal, U.A. (1992, Spring/Summer). Values, Personality and Career Choice. Journal of Applied Social Sciences,16(2),143-59.

Seldon, D. (1985). The Teacher Rebellion. Washington, D.C.: Howard University Press.

Sellars, E. L. (1993, Winter). School Restructuring: Moving From Rhetoric to Reality. Contemporary Education, 64(2), 88-90.

Sergiovanni, T. J. & Starratt, R. J. (1993). Supervision A Redefinition. New York: McGraw-Hill, Inc.

Seron, C. & Ferris, K. (1995, February). Negotiating Professionalism. Work and Occupations,22(1),22-47.

Serow, R. C. (1993, Summer). Why Teach?: Altruism and Career Choice Among Nontraditional Recruits to teaching. Journal of Research and Development in Education, 26(4), 197-204.

Shanker, A. (1988, October). School Change is Union Made. Education Week,5.

Shanker, A. (1989). Reform and the Teaching Profession. In L. Weis, P. G. Altbach, G.P. Kelly, H.G. Petrie, & S. Slaughter (Eds.), Crisis in Teaching: Perspectives on Current Reforms (pp.99-110). Albany, NY: State University of New York Press.

Shanker, A. (April 19, 1993). A Nation Still At Risk. Newsweek, pp. 46-49.

Shanker, A. (Sept. 1, 1993). Restoring the Academic Mission of the School. Vital Speeches 59(22),674-82.

Sharp, W. L. (1992). Collective Negotiations: An Historical Perspective. Journal of Collective Negotiations,21(3), 231-37.

Shea, C. M. (1989). Pentagon vs. Multinational Capitalism: The Political Economy of the 1980's School Reform Movement. In C.M. Shea, E. Kahane, & P. Sola (Eds.), The New Servants of Power: A Critique of the 1980's School Reform Movement (pp. 3-38). New York: Greenwood Press.

Shea, C.M., Kahane, E., Sola, P. (Eds.). (1989). The New Servants of Power: A Critique of the 1980's School Reform Movement. NY: Greenwood Press.

Shedd, J.B. (1988, November). Collective Bargaining, School Reform, and the Management of School Systems. Educational Administration Quarterly, 24(4),405-415.

Sickler, J. (1988). Teachers in Charge: Empowering the Professionals. Phi Delta Kappan,69(5),375-76.

Sirotnik, K.A. (1990). Society, Schooling, Teaching, and Preparing to Teach. In J.I. Goodlad, R. Soder, & K.S. Sirotnik (Eds.), The Moral Dimensions of Teaching (pp. 296-328). San Francisco: Jossey-Bass Publishers.

Sizer, T. R. (1992). School Reform: What's Missing. World Monitor, 5(11), 20-27.

Smith, P. (1990). Killing the Spirit. NY: Viking Penguin Books.

Smylie, M. A. (1991). Organizational Cultures of Schools: Concept, Content, and Change. In S.C. Conley & B.S. Cooper (Eds.), The School as a Work Environment: Implications for School Reform (pp. 20-41). Boston: Allyn & Bacon.

Soder, R. (1990). The Rhetoric of Teacher Professionalization. In J. I. Goodlad, R. Soder, & K.S. Sirotnik (Eds.),The Moral Dimensions of Teaching (pp. 35-86). San Francisco: Jossey-Bass Publishers.

Sommers, N. (1985, May). Collective Bargaining: Is it Time to Dump the Hired Gun? American School Board Journal, 172(5), 29-35.

Sowell, T. (1995). The Vision of the Anointed. New York: Basic Books.

Stieber, J. (1973). Public Employee Unionism: Structure, Growth, Policy. In J.R. Grodin, D.H. Wollett, R.H. Alleyne, Jr.,(Eds.), Collective Bargaining in Public Employment (pp. 17-24). Washington D.C.: The Bureau of National Affairs.

St. John, E.P. (1992). Who Decides Educational Policy? Or How Can the Practitioner Influence Public Choices? In P.F. First, Educational Policy for School Administrators (pp. 96-103). Boston: Allyn & Bacon.

Strike, K.A. (1990). The Legal and Moral Responsibility of Teachers. In John I. Goodlad, R. Soder, & K.S. Sirotnik (Eds.), The Moral Dimensions of Teaching (pp. 188-223). San Francisco: Jossey-Bass Publishers.

Strike, K.A. & Ternasky, P.L. (1993). Ethics in Educational Settings. In K.A. Strike & P.L. Ternasky, (Eds.), Ethics for Professionals in Education (pp. 1-9). New York: Teachers College Press.

Strobel, F.R. (1993). Upward Dreams, Downward Mobility, Lanham, MD: Rowman & Littlefield Publishers, Inc.

Swartz, C.S. (1978). Iowa public school teachers: procedural due process requirements for contract termination. Drake Law Review,28(1), 121-145.

Sykes, G. (1989). Teaching and Professionalism: A Cautionary Perspective. In L. Weis, P.G. Altbach, G.P. Kelly, H.G. Petrie, & S. Slaughter (Eds.), Crisis in Teaching: Perspectives on Current Reforms (pp. 253-273). Albany, NY: State University of New York Press.

Sykes, G. (1990). Fostering Teacher Professionalism in Schools. In R. F. Elmore and Associates, Restructuring Schools (pp. 59-96). San Francisco: Jossey-Bass Publishers.

Sykes, G. (1991). In defense of teacher professionalism as a policy choice. Educational Policy,5, 137-149.

Tamir, Y. (1992). Democracy, Nationalism, and Education. Educational Philosophy and Theory,24(1), 17-27.

Taylor, B. J., & Witney, F. (1992). Labor Relations Law, (6th ed.). Englewood Cliffs, NJ: Prentice Hall.

Thomas, B. R. (1990). The School as a Moral Learning Community. In John I. Goodlad, R. Soder, & K.S. Sirotnik (Eds.), The Moral Dimensions of Teaching (pp. 266-295). San Francisco: Jossey-Bass Publishers.

Thomas, G.J., Sperry, D.J., & Wasden, F.D. (1991). The Law and Teacher Employment. St. Paul: West Publishing Co.

Timar, T.B., & Kirp, D.L. (1988). State Efforts to Reform Schools: Treading Between a Regulatory Swamp and an English Garden. Education Evaluation and Policy Analysis,10(2), 75-88.

Toch, T. (1991). In the Name of Excellence. New York: Oxford University Press.

Tuthill, D. (1990, June). Expanding the Union Contract: One Teacher's Perspective. Phi Delta Kappan,71, 775-780.

Tyler, G. (1976). Why They Organize. In A.M. Cresswell & M.J. Murphy (Eds.), Education and Collective Bargaining (pp. 12-21). Berkeley, CA: McCutchan Publishing Corporation.

Urban, W. J. (1982). Why Teachers Organized. Detroit, MI: Wayne State University Press.

Urban, W.J. (1989). Teacher Activism. In D. Warren, (Ed.). American Teachers: Histories of a Profession at Work (pp. 190-210). New York:Macmillan Publishing Co.

Urban, W. J. (1991, Summer). Is There a New Teacher Unionism? Educational Theory,41(3),331-338.

Valente, W.D. (1994). Law in the Schools (3rd ed.). New York: Macmillan, Inc.

Vander Werf, L.S., Elkin, S.M., Maguire, J.W. (1979). Teacher Militancy and Collective Negotiations. In M.J. Levine & E.C. Hagburg, Labor Relations in the Public Sector (pp. 80-84). Salt Lake City, UT: Brighton Publishing Co.

Van Galen, J. (1987). Maintaining Control: The Structuring of Parent Involvement. In G.W. Noblit & W.T. Pink, Schooling in Social Context(pp.78-90). Norwood, NJ: Ablex Publishing Corporation.

van Geel, T. (1987). The Courts and American Education Law. Buffalo, NY: Prometheus Books.

Van Hoy, J. (1993, February). Intraprofessional Politics and Professional Regulation. Work and Occupations, 20(1), 90-111.

Van Maanan, J., & Barley, S.R. (1984). Occupational Communities: Culture and control in organizations. Research in Organizational Behavior,6, 287-365.

Walker, P.A., & Roder, L. (1993, Spring). Reflections on the Practical and Legal Implications of School-Based Management and Teacher Empowerment. Journal of Law & Education,22(2),159-75.

Walter, R.L. (1975). Teacher and Collective Bargaining. Lincoln, NE: Professional Educators Publications, Inc.

Walzer, M. (1983). Spheres of Justice. New York: Basic Books, Inc.

Wanat, C.L., Helms,L., Engvall,R. (1994,September). Parents Versus Teachers: Avoiding Litigation in an Era of Greater Community Involvement. People and Education,2(3), pp. 320-337.

Warren, D. (Ed.). (1989). American Teachers: Histories of a Profession at Work. New York: Macmillan Publishing Co.

Wasley, P. A. (1991). Teachers Who Lead. New York: Teachers College Press.

Webb, J.F. (1989). A Decade After Commonwealth v. County Board of Arlington:Public Employee Bargaining in Virginia Reconsidered .Journal of Collective Negotiations in the Public Sector,18(1), 59-71.

Weber, A.R. (1977). Prospects for the Future. In J.R. Grodin, D.H. Wollett, R.H. Alleyne, Jr, Collective Bargaining in Public Employment (pp. 1-8). Washington, D.C.: The Bureau of National Affairs, Inc.

Webster, W.G., Sr. (1985). Effective Collective Bargaining in Public Education. Ames, IA: Iowa State University Press.

Weick, K. (1976). Educational organizations as loosely coupled systems. Administrative Science Quarterly, 21(1), 1-19.

Weick, K. (1982, June). Administrating education in loosely coupled schools. Phi Delta Kappan,63(10),673-676.

Weiler, P. and Mundlak, G. (1993, June). New Directions for the Law of the Workplace. Yale Law Journal,102(8),1907-1925.

Weimer, M. (1993). Improving Your Classroom Teaching. Newbury Park, CA: Sage Publications, Inc.

Weis, L., Altbach, P.G., Kelly, G.P., Petrie, H.G., Slaughter, S. (Eds.). (1989). Crisis in Teaching: Perspectives on Current Reforms. Albany, NY: State University of New York Press.

Weisberger, J.M., (1977). The Appropriate Scope of Bargaining in the Public Sector: The Continuing Controversy and the Wisconsin Experience. Wisconsin Law Review,1977(3),685-745.

Weiss, C.H. (1993, Fall). Shared Decision Making About What? A Comparison of Schools with and without Teacher Participation. Teachers College Record,95(1),69-92.

Wiles, J. & Bondi, J. (1985). The School Board Primer. Boston: Allyn and Bacon, Inc.

Wise, A.E., & Leibbrand, J. (1993, October). Accreditation and the Creation of a Profession of Teaching. Phi Delta Kappan, 75(2), 133-157.

Wise, R.I. (1981). Schools, businesses, and educational needs: From cooperation to collaboration. Education and Urban Society,14(1), 67-82.

Wishnick, Y. S., & Wishnick, T. K. (1993). Collective Bargaining and Educational Reform: Establishing a Labor-Management Partnership. Journal of Collective Negotiations in the Public Sector, 22(1), 1-12.

Wood, G.H. (1992). Schools That Work. New York: Penguin Books.

Worster, R. (1993, September). Still Fighting Yesterday's Battle. Newsweek, p. 12.

Zerger, K.L. (1988, Summer). Teacher Evaluation and Collective Bargaining: A Union Perspective. Journal of Law and Education, 17(3), 507-25.